D1368327

THE EXECUTIVE CHECKLIST

A GUIDE FOR SETTING DIRECTION
AND MANAGING CHANGE

JAMES M. KERR

palgrave
macmillan

First published in 2014 by
PALGRAVE MACMILLAN®
in the United States—a division of St. Martin's Press LLC,
175 Fifth Avenue, New York, NY 10010.

Where this book is distributed in the UK, Europe and the rest of the world,
this is by Palgrave Macmillan, a division of Macmillan Publishers Limited,
registered in England, company number 785998, of Houndmills,
Basingstoke, Hampshire RG21 6XS.

Palgrave Macmillan is the global academic imprint of the above companies
and has companies and representatives throughout the world.

Palgrave® and Macmillan® are registered trademarks in the United States,
the United Kingdom, Europe and other countries.

ISBN: 978–1–137–33743–6

Library of Congress Cataloging-in-Publication Data

Kerr, James M.
    The executive checklist : a guide for setting direction and managing
    change / James M. Kerr.
        pages cm
        ISBN 978–1–137–33743–6 (alk. paper)
        1. Organizational change. 2. Organizational effectiveness. 3. Strategic
    planning. 4. Industrial management. I. Title.

HD58.8.K4667 2014
658.4′063—dc23   2013023118

A catalogue record of the book is available from the British Library.

Design by Newgen Knowledge Works (P) Ltd., Chennai, India.

First edition: January 2014

10 9 8 7 6 5 4 3 2 1

Printed in the United States of America.

CONTENTS

Acknowledgments   ix

OPENING REMARKS   The Executive Checklist Can Make the
                   Business World a Little Simpler   1

CHAPTER 1   Establish Leadership—The Foundation
                   for Change   5

CHAPTER 2   Build Trust—A Vital Component of
                   Enduring Achievement   25

CHAPTER 3   Strategy Setting—Translating Vision
                   into Action   45

CHAPTER 4   Engage Staff—The Way to Gain Support
                   and Accelerate Success   67

CHAPTER 5   Manage Work through Projects—A Means
                   to Strategic Alignment   87

CHAPTER 6   Renovate the Business—A Way to Become
                   "of Choice"   109

CHAPTER 7   Align Technology—It's at the Core of
                   All We Do   129

CHAPTER 8   Transform Staff—The People Part of
                   Enterprise-wide Change   149

CHAPTER 9   Renew Communications Practices—
                   Transparency Improves Performance   169

CHAPTER 10   Reimagine the Organization—The
                   Expressway to the Future   189

POSTSCRIPT A Bold Vision for Tomorrow's Organizations   209

A Last Word   213

About the Author   215

Notes   217

Index   221

ACKNOWLEDGMENTS

To the people who made a difference to me while I was writing this book, especially

Irene, Dylan, and Haley—you give my effort meaning;

my extended family, including the in-laws and my Cromwell friends who are always there when I need them;

Brian McCarthy and Joe Buyak, who regularly helped me clear my head and gain perspective;

my agent, Giles Anderson, who believed in the project from its inception and found a good home for the book;

my editor at Palgrave Macmillan, Laurie Harting, and her entire team, who encouraged me to do my best, while they did the rest; and

all of my clients over the years who continue to provide me with ample opportunities to learn and grow as I hone my craft.

Thank you.

THE EXECUTIVE CHECKLIST CAN MAKE THE BUSINESS WORLD A LITTLE SIMPLER

The beginning is the most important part of the work.
—Plato

Today's business world is extremely complex and challenging. It's easy for even the most seasoned executive to make a mistake or overlook a detail that can lead to utter failure for his or her business. This book is about keeping it simple.

What better way to simplify the complex than to create a checklist? Checklists are a modest way to reduce failure, ensure consistency, and safeguard comprehensiveness. They're used everywhere—from Mom's grocery list to Dad's "To Do" list.

But did you know that checklists support very sophisticated and important processes and activities, as well? There are preflight checklists used by commercial pilots, surgical safety checklists used by neurosurgeons, and structural engineering checklists used by bridge-builders. These things save lives. It doesn't get much more important than that!

So, why not devise a checklist for business executives, too?

WHY AN EXECUTIVE CHECKLIST?

We have entered a new commercial age. The business models from the past that relied heavily on size and leverage will no longer deliver returns. Clearly, regulatory restructuring on a global scale is underway. Transparency is being demanded from all quarters, which is thus reconstituting the way businesses are run. In turn, all of this change is informing the design and evolution of the millennium's new economy.

As a result, executives are being tasked to optimize their enterprise's organizational structures, to enhance product and service delivery models, and to blaze new paths to unmatched market reach. This is not a trivial task in and of itself, but add to that the "need for speed," driven by the continued advancement of technological capabilities, and this generation of business executives just may be facing the greatest management challenge of the postindustrial era.

There's just so much to demystify, understand, leverage, manage, and coordinate in order to build an organization that is ever prepared to do what it takes to respond to a rapidly shifting and, often, disorganized world economy. Today's enterprises must be swift to change, skillful in service delivery, and virtually interconnected across a value chain that, more often than not, spans the globe.

To be successful in this extremely complex and unstable business environment, executive leaders must do all that they can to simplify. Therefore, checklists are in order.

CHECKLISTS MAKE LIFE EASIER

This book is a result of my quest to streamline the work of my executive clients. One can say that the book has been decades in the making. As my management consulting practice enters its third decade, I have had occasion to reflect back on the terrific engagements that I have had with some of the largest, most successful enterprises in the world. It is through work with clients like IBM, The Home Depot, and JP Morgan Chase that I have enjoyed the unique opportunity to witness, firsthand, the economic changes and organizational challenges that have led us to where we are today.

Indeed, it is through rich, client experiences that *The Executive Checklist* was born. I found that, regardless of industry, company size, or financials, every executive with whom I have worked over the years can follow this checklist and fashion the type of organization that is needed to flourish in the new millennium.

THE EXECUTIVE CHECKLIST

Here is The Executive Checklist:

✓ Establish Leadership
✓ Build Trust
✓ Set Strategy
✓ Engage Staff
✓ Manage Work as Projects
✓ Renovate the Business
✓ Align Technology
✓ Transform Staff
✓ Renew Communications Practices
✓ Reimagine Organizational Design

At first glance, these ten items seem innocuous enough. However, there is a great deal of meaning and relevance packed into each item on the list. None of them should be taken lightly.

Certainly, the approach to how a given manager performs or oversees each checklist item and the results that are garnered from the effort will vary greatly and be influenced by all sorts of variables that are unique to an organization and a manager's experience.

However, be warned that each of these checklist items must be attended to thoughtfully in order to position an enterprise for continued success into the future. *The Executive Checklist* provides a framework to be used to institute overarching, enterprise-wide transformation.

HOW THE BOOK IS ORGANIZED

We will explore each of the checklist items in more detail within the book. In fact, there is a corresponding chapter and supplementary checklist dedicated to each one. The resulting collection of checklists serves as a primer for how to best oversee and lead a twenty-first-century organization into the future. The sidebars (labeled *See It in Action*) presented in each chapter provide important examples of key checklist concepts that are already being applied in businesses today.

The reader can approach the material by reading the book from beginning to end. However, by presenting the material in a checklist format, the book can be used as a quick reference guide, as well. This allows the reader to skip to the chapters that most interest him or her and to explore only the ideas related to a particular checklist topic.

This feature may be particularly useful for those readers who are junior executives or those only recently promoted to the management ranks, who may only be concerned with learning about a specific topic for which they are newly responsible.

Whatever way one chooses to use the book, that is up to him or her. The intention is to provide insights into the vital elements needed to drive and manage the change required to reposition today's businesses for a successful tomorrow, while making access to the information available within the book as straightforward as possible.

Read on and see how *The Executive Checklist* makes today ultracomplex business world a little easier to manage.

1

ESTABLISH LEADERSHIP—THE FOUNDATION FOR CHANGE

If your actions inspire others to dream more, learn more, do more and become more, you are a leader.

—John Quincy Adams

It's been said that outstanding leaders lead by example. This means that they demonstrate desired qualities and behaviors to their teams through their actions and conduct. By doing so, these leaders put forth a sense that they and their staffs share the same goals and aspirations and that together, they are going to go about achieving these ambitions as one team.

Forming this type of leadership—in which everyone within an organization feels as though he or she is working toward a common good—is essential to the achievement of every other concept presented in the book. Indeed, establishing leadership is the foundation for change. Without it, any attempt to institute sweeping organizational transformation becomes wasted effort. It is for this reason that the need to establish leadership is at the top of the *Executive Checklist*.

So, let's examine what it takes to establish leadership within an enterprise. The following checklist outlines the key elements in forming the leadership foundation required to set direction and manage change:

Leadership Establishment Checklist

✓ Have a Dream

✓ Actively Set Direction

✓ Communicate Early and Often

✓ Be Dynamic and Visibly Involved

✓ Promote Collaboration

✓ Practice Inclusiveness

✓ Don't Tolerate Bad Leaders in Your Midst

✓ Make No Excuses

Let's review these checklist items in the context of establishing the leadership foundation that is needed for change.

CHECKLIST ITEM 1: HAVE A DREAM

Corporate transformation begins with a dream. It provides the context for every other change concept or improvement initiative that will follow. It is a leader's responsibility to dream the dream and reimagine what the organization is about and how it will conduct its affairs and execute its mission well into the future. This responsibility holds true whether one is envisioning a new direction for a global concern or redefining the work environment at the division level.

The dream, or vision, must become the stuff of rallying cries and express the common goal that the leader and team will share. Once the vision is defined, the leader must articulate it and spread the message across the enterprise. This must be done in such a way that every staff member can understand and buy into the dream.

The methods used to socialize the vision can vary. Town hall meetings and so forth are commonly used to promote the vision and engage personnel. However, I've found that there are better ways to create some energy around the sharing of the dream. I worked with several companies to design and stage a Vision Trade Show for their staff as a means of getting the message out. See *Let's Have a Vision Trade Show* for a description of the method that was used at LexisNexis.

See It in Action

Let's Have a Vision Trade Show

When LexisNexis Insurance Software division developed its vision story, we chose an innovative way to socialize it among staff members—by conducting a Vision Trade Show.

Held in several sessions over the course of a few days, employees were randomly divided into small groups. Each group was assigned a specific trade show booth at which to meet for the commencement of the trade show. At designated time intervals, groups were asked to rotate to the next booth.

Each booth was hosted by a member of the senior leadership team. Once at a booth, staff members were treated to a briefing or demonstration highlighting a specific element of the firm's vision story. To make the trade show experience even more realistic, each booth provided attendees with various giveaways including logowear, squeeze balls, and golf goodie bags.

The trade show booth format lent itself naturally to the presentation of key vision story themes and the emphasis of important points, like speed to market, continual transformation, and the building of a talent factory. Management's commitment to the vision was easily demonstrated through each leader's willingness to "man" the booth and deliver his or her part of the vision story throughout the day.

The event, along with its accompanying "Vision Magazine," which was used to document and convey the division's vision story (for more on that, see *The LexisNexis Vision Magazine*, in Chapter 3), was indispensable in helping staff members understand the firm's vision and gaining their engagement in the process of making it a reality.

Clearly, it takes deliberate effort to enable every employee to understand the vision and to feel a sense of sharing in its common purpose. When that is achieved, however, there is a very strong sense that everyone is in it together and committed to doing the work needed to achieve that purpose.

We will talk more about visioning and its relationship to strategy setting (another essential Executive Checklist topic) in Chapter 3. For now, let it suffice to say that leadership is gained by, first, dreaming a dream and sharing it with the troops in the trenches. After all, people can't follow what they don't understand.

Indeed, leadership begins with socializing the dream for the future. All layers of management participate in this work in important ways, from the executive who dreams the dream to the middle managers who translate the dream, to the supervisory layer that works with staff members to realize the dream.

CHECKLIST ITEM 2: ACTIVELY SET DIRECTION

Leadership is gained and followership is multiplied through active direction-setting. It's one thing to dream the dream and communicate it—it's another to achieve it. A strategic plan that serves as a game plan for execution must be built to support the achievement of the vision. However, putting a strategic plan in place without involved oversight and direction-setting from the top will not suffice.

Indeed, an executive must be fully engaged, monitor progress. and chart the course of action throughout all of the plan's execution activities. It is equally important that new and improved ideas be folded into the plan as appropriate, and that midcourse adjustments be made in a timely and efficient way, thus improving the odds for long-term success.

Here are some ways in which executives can ensure that they have the opportunity to actively set direction and fine-tune the strategic plan:

✓ **Map Strategic Work against Its Contribution to the Vision—**
   Understanding what each strategic initiative is intended to deliver and how those deliverables contribute to the achievement of the vision is an essential element of setting direction and managing change. By always drawing a connection that clearly shows how a proposed initiative will lead to vision attainment, a de facto evaluation screen for

new ideas is established—one for which the "acid test" is an initiative's intended contribution to achieving the vision.

If the "acid test" indicates that a given initiative is faltering or showing signs that it will not deliver on expected results, then expectations can be reexamined and actions can be taken to redirect assets as necessary, either fortifying the project for success or closing it down before it squanders additional resources.

✓ **Launch Plan Administration Function**—In essence, the plan administration function manages the mechanics behind the refinement and execution of the strategic plan. It does this by coordinating the regular review and update of the organization's strategic plan with the senior management team. This is another vehicle that executives can institute in order to make appropriate midcourse adjustments. Specifically, a plan administration function is responsible for:

   ✓ Putting the processes in place to ensure executive ownership of the Strategic Plan;
   ✓ Updating the firm's strategic plan per the direction of the executive team; and,
   ✓ Providing proper support to project managers and their teams as they execute strategic initiatives.

Clearly, it is no small task to institutionalize plan administration within a concern. This can take the form of one person being assigned the responsibility, or a small unit can be established to drive the processes of plan administration. Regardless, the function provides a very important means of ensuring that executives remain active in strategic planning.

✓ **Institute Management Huddles**—Think of a management huddle as an official "time out" from the daily grind of managing the operation. Called, as needed, by an executive when an unexpected problem arises, management huddles gather key managers and select subject matter experts together to engage in immediate problem-solving and action planning.

Management huddles provide a straightforward way to communicate important information between an executive and his or her management team in a timely manner. The practice bypasses standing meetings and other progress monitoring / reporting processes that might be in place. It is a handy way to swiftly cut to the chase when a potentially damaging issue is escalating within the organization.

Be careful not to use this technique too much. Too many huddles can add unnecessary drama to the workplace and give the team a sense that the business is out of control. Management huddles should be applied only when immediate action is necessary and the resolution of the issue cannot wait for a regularly scheduled meeting or standing review session.

When used judiciously, management huddles become an important tool that is at an executive's disposal for dynamically providing the leadership necessary to avert a crisis.

CHECKLIST ITEM 3: COMMUNICATE EARLY AND OFTEN

Leaders cannot communicate enough with their organizations. People want to have a shared sense of belonging and develop a feeling that everyone in the organization is working toward the same end. Communication is an important part of engaging and uniting people in working toward the common goal as set forth in the vision.

However, communications must be kept simple and consistent. If there is any sense that information is being withheld or that the facts are being manipulated within the work setting, then all bets are off. People will simply not trust the information that they are getting and will not feel like they share in that common goal. Therefore, as the saying goes, communicate early and often.

Here are a few tried-and-true techniques that can be used to ensure that hands-on communication gets woven into the work culture:

✓ **Schedule Ad-Hoc Manager and Supervisor One-on-Ones:** It's a good idea to build a solid rapport with the management team—even those several levels below. Once trust is established, a senior leader will likely get a more unbiased and balanced point of view of what's going on within the enterprise than he or she might get from his or her own direct reports, and the unfiltered communication will likely enable more timely and effective leadership on his or her part.

✓ **Do "Drive-Bys":** There's no need for a senior leader to limit his or her interactions to managers and supervisors. He or she should visit with his or her team within their work units, discuss changes that they are involved in, and ask for their opinions on how to make things better. This type of "management by walking around" can go a long way toward improving an executive's understanding of where his or her workers are, both emotionally and intellectually.

✓ **Institute an Overall Program Coordination Process:** Organizationally, a firm is well advised to establish a formal program coordination process. Such a process ensures that the project managers responsible for each change initiative meet on a regular basis to discuss progress, share cross-project work, and brainstorm solutions to nagging problems that can wreak havoc on a complex and multifaceted program. Occasional attendance at project coordination meetings will improve communication with the people doing the work and can help an executive to better steer the change effort toward success.

✓ **Build Regular Sponsor Review Meetings into Each Change Initiative:** A principal way in which a leader can improve communications with the people who are driving change for him or her is by regularly reviewing status and understanding the challenges that these people and their teams are facing as they manage through these initiatives. It's important to build regularly scheduled sponsor review sessions into project / program plans. This provides leaders with ample opportunities to communicate and to lead.

✓ **Demand and Review Weekly Status Reports:** It's important for project teams to regularly document project status. Weekly project reports are particularly helpful to executive sponsors in tracking progress during the "in-between times" amid sponsor review meetings. In the event that intervention is needed on an off-week, action can be taken.

Furthermore, leaders can demonstrate their commitment to the corporate change effort by simply commenting back on a status report. Can you imagine the impact on a junior executive who receives some kind words from a senior leader? It gives the junior executive confirmation and inspires him or her to double-down on his or her commitment to the effort.

It is a good idea to establish a standard form to report weekly project status. This promotes consistency and accelerates understanding of issues.

✓ **Keep Your Door Wide Open:** Finally, executives need to practice an open-door policy (especially for key project managers and teams). By making it simple for team participants to approach a senior leader and discuss issues, a winning atmosphere is created that will spill over to the entire enterprise.

Once you institute this policy, make sure that you mean it. If an executive claims to have an open-door policy, yet makes it difficult for staff members to reach out to him or her, then morale will certainly be sabotaged and the executive's leadership questioned.

Communication plays a vital role when establishing leadership. If they approach communication the right way, executives can demonstrate their commitment to their people through active communication. For more on communication, check out Chapter 9, which is a vital Executive Checklist topic in its own right.

CHECKLIST ITEM 4: BE DYNAMIC AND VISIBLY INVOLVED

With the proper communication elements in place that provide hands-on opportunities for executive involvement, it is important that leaders take the opportunity to be involved and provide proactive, dynamic coaching of their people. A dynamic coach is active, directive, and forceful. The coach understands his or her team by being involved and active in their work, and can provide the "right" touch at the "right" time—being directive when the path to success is unclear and being supportive when it's time to empower the team.

Teams charged with effecting change usually begin their work together ardently. They are eager and energized by the new assignment. However, when the freshness of the new initiative begins to turn stale, a team can falter and its productivity decline. It is here that clear direction is needed. It is here that an executive can provide the dynamic coaching required, helping the team blow through its roadblocks and continue down the path to success.

If a team does not receive the active, directive leadership required to propel it forward, it will stall and flounder—unsure of what to do or how to do it. Make no mistake, people need dynamic coaching and active leadership on significant and new change initiatives. Such leadership can make or break a transformation program. Take a moment to read *CIGNA's Transformation Failure* for more on what can happen to transformation programs that lack dynamic leadership.

With senior leaders becoming more active and directive (providing teams with the dynamic coaching and support that they need, when they need it), project teams can become enormously productive—facilitating great change of vast impact. Direct, active executive leadership in change management work not only brings about significant improvement but also contributes to employee engagement and commitment.

See It in Action

CIGNA's Transformation Failure

"Unfortunately, we have not executed well [on transformation]," confessed Patrick Welch, the new president of CIGNA HealthCare, to investors on Oct. 28, 2002. *"The cost is greater than anticipated, much of the economic and service benefits are yet to be realized, and transformation shortfalls have led to service shortfalls, which have led to lower new sales and [customer] retention."*

Welch is referring to the fallout from CIGNA's failed transformation effort –aimed at leveraging information technology to streamline service delivery and improve the consumer experience—that turned customers away in droves and took a severe toll on the insurance carrier's bottom line.

The executives responsible for the transformation program chose to use a leading systems integrator and management consulting firm to drive the change management and business process improvements, as well as to develop and implement the new customer facing applications that would allow members to enroll online, choose health plan options, change benefit selections, check claims status, and review plan details.

Unfortunately for all concerned, the leadership was too far removed from the details to understand the ramifications of being too aggressive in seeking the benefits from the transformation program. Instead of adequately vetting the new systems and processes over a period of time, the executives involved impulsively eliminated the 3,100 customer service representatives upon delivery of the new system. Pandemonium summarily broke out.

Here is some of what ensued:

✓ Some insured customers were denied coverage;
✓ New enrollment cards could not be issued;
✓ Replacement ID numbers were issued incorrectly;
✓ Prescription coverage information was recorded inaccurately, leading to coverage denial;
✓ Calls swamped the recently downsized customer service centers;
✓ Customers were lost to competitors.

Certainly, much has improved over time at CIGNA.

Clearly, the debacle that occurred at CIGNA during the early stages of the healthcare crisis in the United States serves as a solid reminder of how bad the situation can become when leaders fail to lead. The subject of many a business school case study ever since, what happened at CIGNA illustrates what can occur when leaders are too far removed from the details of their operations to adequately anticipate trouble and proactively manage risk.

Sure, all of the senior leaders involved with the fiasco, from Patrick Welch on down to Heyward Donigan, the senior vice president of service operations and the executive in-charge of the transformation program, are no longer at the company as a result. However, that does little in the way of recouping the millions lost or repairing the damage done to the company.

In fact, according to last year's 2012 Temkin Ratings (the Temkin Ratings uses feedback collected from consumers to evaluate organizations and provide insights into how large organizations treat their customers), CIGNA still ranked in the lowest 10 percent in both consumer trust and client loyalty and, more interestingly, the insurer was in the lowest 5 percent in customer-support satisfaction.

All of this begs the question *"How long does it take a firm to heal from the wounds exacted by poor leadership?"*

Sources:

1) "Cigna's Self-Inflicted Wounds," Alison Bass, *CIO Magazine*, May 15, 2003.

2) http://www.temkinratings.com/, January 2013.

CHECKLIST ITEM 5: PROMOTE COLLABORATION

Collaboration is a foundation stone on which an organization can be built into an unstoppable powerhouse. When people work cooperatively with others, they gain confidence in their individual abilities to handle any situation—a trait every executive wants in his or her personnel.

Unmistakably, the setting of a collaborative tone within an organization starts at the top. Staff members emulate the behavior of their leaders. If the leader seeks out opinions and solicits input, then his or her personnel will naturally understand that this type of behavior is also expected of them. A collaborative work environment can be established by an executive who collaborates with subordinates.

This is an important element of establishing leadership, too. Teamwork and collaboration must be built to enable the inspired enthusiasm necessary to transform an organization. That said, executives must recognize and celebrate collaborative behavior and extinguish selfish and egocentric conduct. Otherwise, self-serving and other undesirable behaviors are likely to tiptoe into the organization, undermining leadership and sabotaging the change effort. Read about one of the ways in which Steve Jobs promoted collaboration in *Pixar: Collaboration in the Atrium.*

See It in Action

Pixar: Collaboration in the Atrium

Alienus Non Diutius—Roughly translated from Latin, it means "alone no longer."

The words are emblazoned on the crest of Pixar University, the professional development center and training ground for employees of Pixar Studios. The motto is fitting for an organization whose cofounder, Steve Jobs, believed in the power and significance of collaboration. He even made sure that the very building housing the studio's 700-plus employees was designed in such a way as to promote collaboration among all of the professionals who inhabit the complex.

He is quoted as saying, *"If a building doesn't encourage [collaboration], you'll lose a lot of innovation and the magic that's sparked by serendipity. So we designed the building to make people get out of their offices and mingle in the central atrium with people they might not otherwise see."*

Accordingly, Jobs insisted that the meeting rooms, the cafeteria, the coffee bar, the gift shop, and even employee mailboxes all be designed as part of the atrium. He wanted to ensure that different work groups, from animators to programmers to art directors, all had the opportunity to mingle together to share ideas and collaborate.

The proof is in the pudding. Pixar went on to revolutionize filmmaking—proving that computers and animation can do as equally compelling a job of engaging a movie audience as actors and cameras can. Even today, under the Disney moniker, the firm continues to win awards (the studio has earned 26 Academy Awards, 7 Golden Globe Awards, and 11 Grammy Awards), while increasing high-quality production output and fending off the advances of competitors like DreamWorks and other aggressive upstarts, proving that deliberate collaboration matters and can make a difference in the long-term success of an enterprise.

Source: http://www.newyorker.com/online/blogs/newsdesk/2011/10/steve -jobs-pixar.html, *October 7, 2011.*

CHECKLIST ITEM 6: PRACTICE INCLUSIVENESS

Leaders must demonstrate inclusive behavior. This is done by including staff in key meetings and engaging team members in discussion. This inclusiveness provides a platform for soliciting and sharing insights, and conveying important information as long as differences of opinion are recognized and valued.

Keep in mind, inclusiveness must be exhibited, not just talked about. Coworkers know the difference. I've worked with several business leaders over the years who characterized themselves as being inclusive, but who rarely solicited opinions or valued different points of view.

Conversely, I've helped clients establish inclusive environments that leveraged the best ideas regardless of their source. Executives have to create work settings that routinely dig deep into the organization to solicit and cultivate the best and brightest ideas from every staff member—it's the best way to get the best answers to today's business challenges. It's also the best way for an executive to establish leadership among all employees (see *Forbes Insight's Diversity & Inclusion Survey* for more interesting perspectives on the importance of inclusive leadership).

See It in Action

Forbes Insight's Diversity & Inclusion Survey

In summer 2011, Forbes Insights conducted a comprehensive survey of more than 300 senior executives from around the globe. The companies that these executives represented had revenues of at least

$500 million, and went up to more than $20 billion. Here are the key findings from the survey:

✓ **Diversity is a key driver of innovation, and is a critical component of a company's being successful on a global scale.** Senior executives are recognizing that a diverse set of experiences, perspectives, and backgrounds is crucial to innovation and the development of new ideas. When asked about the relationship between diversity and innovation, a majority of respondents agreed that diversity is crucial to encouraging different perspectives and ideas that foster innovation.

✓ **A diverse and inclusive workforce is crucial for companies that want to attract and retain top talent.** Competition for talent is fierce in today's global economy, so companies need to have plans in place to recruit, develop, and retain a diverse workforce.

✓ **Nearly all respondents reported that their companies have diversity and inclusion strategies in place.** However, not all of the plans are identical. About a third said their companies have global strategies that allow for minimal regional deviation, while half said that their organizations have a global plan that also allows for different strategies and programs in order to address regional needs or cultural differences.

✓ **Organizations' diversity goals and priorities won't change significantly over the next three years.** When asked about their company's current diversity and inclusion priorities, 43 percent cited retention and development of talent, followed by ensuring diversity in the workplace in general (35 percent), developing a robust pipeline of diverse talent (29 percent), and managing cross-generational issues (28 percent).

✓ **Responsibility for the success of company's diversity/ inclusion efforts lies with senior management.** In order for a diversity/inclusion plan to have real meaning, there needs to be accountability and oversight. Seven out of ten companies reported that the buck stops at the C-level and their board of directors.

✓ **Significant progress has been made to build and retain diverse workforces, but there are still some impediments to companies' efforts.** Respondents feel they've made progress in gender diversity, but they feel they've fallen short in areas such as disability and age.

As these survey results indicate, inclusion is an important success factor for business. It provides obvious benefits for organizations that embrace and institutionalize inclusive behavior. It is up to us as leaders to drive it through action into the organizations that we influence.

Source: *Global Diversity and Inclusion: Fostering Innovation through a Diverse Workforce by Forbes Insight,* www.forbesmedia.com, *July 12, 2011.*

CHECKLIST ITEM 7: DON'T TOLERATE
BAD LEADERS IN YOUR MIDST

A bad leader can wreak havoc on an organization. They can cripple morale and undermine a senior executive's agenda. Therefore, an executive seeking to establish leadership within an organization should never tolerate bad subordinate managers for whom they are responsible. That said, they need to identify poor leadership and do whatever is required to correct or eliminate it, for to tolerate the behavior of terrible leaders only sends the unwelcome message to underlings that such behavior is condoned.

While bad leaders can take many forms and share many interconnecting characteristics, there are six primary types to recognize and eradicate:

1. **The Micro-Manager**—whose insecurities are so great that he or she cannot possibly trust that anyone can do anything without his or her superior guidance. These managers tend to be control freaks who orchestrate every move within their area of responsibility, stifling the creativity and independence of those who work for them.

    This type of leader is widely disliked and resented. But, his or her frail ego prohibits the leader from recognizing this fact. These leaders prefer, instead, to think of themselves as being highly respected by peers and subordinates for their incredible competence. The result of this leadership style is a highly dysfunctional organization whose staff are paralyzed to take action for fear of reprisal.

2. **The Slave Driver**—who knows no limit to human effort. This type of leader has no work/home life balance, and they assume that their subordinates need no balance in their lives either. Nonetheless, the Slave Driver advances onward, leaving countless casualties in his or her wake.

    Burnout among the rank and file distinguishes work units managed by the Slave Driver type. These units are not a fun place to work, and long hours contribute to the problem. True discontent sets in, however, when personnel realize that there's no relief in sight. Clearly, this way of managing people is toxic, and it poisons all those inhabiting the work environment.

3. **The Bully**—who uses threats and intimidation in order to attain his or her ambitions. Bullies tend be brash and dominating, adopting a dismissive demeanor to hide a frail and delicate ego, one that neither seeks out collaborative contributions nor tolerates any feedback that smacks of criticism.

    An organization becomes boorish in its thinking and behavior with a Bully in command. Cut-throat behavior becomes the norm. Everyone is out for him- or herself, knowing that there's no reward for being a "good guy." In fact, Bullies often drive away solid contributors who can't tolerate being mistreated, leaving behind only those who lack the confidence or skills to find a better job somewhere else.

4. **The Egomaniac**—who is incapable of recognizing any contribution that a subordinate provides and is willing to steal credit for a job well done from the people that work for them. Driven by a deep-rooted belief that the world revolves around them, this type of leader views his or her staff as expendable pawns, there only to serve the Egomaniac.

    A department led by an Egomaniac is likely typified by an uninspired and apathetic workforce that does the bare minimum and nothing more. It doesn't take long for workers in Egomaniac-led business areas to understand that their extra effort will never be recognized or rewarded, regardless of the benefit that it provides the enterprise. Therefore, few commit to doing anything more than is required.

5. **The Deceiver**—who has no conscience. These leaders are very comfortable using deception to get ahead. They routinely deliver misleading information and make empty promises in order to cheat customers and deceive staff members. Indeed, their message comes across loud and clear to all in the organization through their commands and deeds.

 Chaos can result in a work unit led by a Deceiver, because there is no order where dishonesty is part of the business framework. How can you establish order when misinformation has been woven into the corporate culture? Where is the boundary line drawn when personnel are taught that cheating is a fine business practice as long as it helps further the cause? It can be a recipe for pure pandemonium because no one can discern reality from fiction.

6. **The Mad Scientist**—who has no true commitment to the organizations that employ him or her. These leaders see business as one big test tube in which to perform experiments and develop new ideas for use at their next job. Oftentimes, this type of leader will simply walk away and find another place to set up shop.

 Because Mad Scientists are indifferent to any negative fallout that results from an experiment gone wrong, the organizations that they run are often marked by confusion and instability. Consequently, it can take years to reestablish an organization ravaged by the Mad Scientist-leader whose uncalculated risk-taking has leveled an enterprise, leaving it an unrecognizable wasteland.

 Plainly, an executive seeking to establish leadership cannot afford to let any of these types of leaders flourish within his or her ranks. The devastating damage that can be done by one bad leader in a key position cannot be underestimated. It is an executive's responsibility to take whatever action necessary to remove or rehabilitate bad leaders and create a satisfying work setting that inspires and motivates everyone in the organization.

CHECKLIST ITEM 8: MAKE NO EXCUSES

If a leader is to hold his or her team to a high standard, then he or she must be held to the same. No excuses for bad behavior or poor performance should be made or deemed acceptable. It's a simple formula, but one that can transform if applied in an open and honest way.

Leaders cannot make excuses for their own shortcomings or failures if they want people to follow them. I've witnessed leaders who routinely make excuses for their less than exemplary conduct—it turns people off and it serves to dispirit subordinates who have to endure the endless justifications.

Executives must strive to establish an organization in which they and their staff act as one. There is an all-pervading sense within such companies that every employee, from the chief executive officer to the cleaning crew who sweeps the floors at night, shares common goals, communicates with each other in timely and effective ways, and always acts as one. Take a look at *Making No Excuses at Virgin* for an example of the concept in action.

See It in Action

Making No Excuses at Virgin

Richard Branson cofounded what was to become one of the biggest independent record labels in the world. Through great vision, hard work, and shrewd maneuvering and risk-taking he transformed Virgin Records into a huge, transnational corporation comprising lifestyle, media, money, music, and environmental and travel businesses that span the globe.

But that type of success doesn't just happen. Branson consistently walked the talk and took the responsibility for leading his company through all of its ups and downs—epitomizing the meaning of the "buck stops here." It is seldom difficult to take credit when things are going along swimmingly. It is a far greater challenge to shoulder accountability when things don't go so well.

Over the years, some of Virgin's businesses have flopped. Remember Virgin Cola? It failed to usurp Coca-Cola as the world's favorite soft drink. It's no longer around. How about Virgin Digital? It was intended to rival iTunes. It didn't make it, either. Even in failure, though, Branson never played the blame game. He took responsibility for decisions made and risks taken and moved on.

When an executive leader operates in this fashion and makes no excuses for poor performance or failure, he or she fosters accountability in everyone who works for him or her. In such organizations, everyone is in it together—equally learning from failures and celebrating the wins. It becomes a winning organization, just like Virgin.

IN CLOSING

The work of the executive begins by establishing the leadership necessary to inspire and guide the organization to unbridled success.

In fact, the most outstanding leaders convey a very strong sense of being "in it together" among the people whom they lead. They collaborate with and include staff in problem-solving and issue adjudication. The best executives don't pretend to have all of the answers. Rather, they prefer to solicit input and perspectives from the front-line personnel who do the work every day.

It should be mentioned that exceptional leadership can be undermined, however, if the executive in charge tolerates bad behavior within his or her management team. It is an executive's responsibility to do away with bad behavior and demand that the management team work and act as one—all of the time, no excuses.

Great leaders transform. They not only revitalize the organizations in which they work, but they invigorate the people with whom they work. They do this by dreaming the dream, widely communicating it, and making it their business to be keenly involved in the achievement of their vision through dynamic direction-setting.

In the next chapter, we will explore the second key item on the *Executive Checklist*—the importance of building trust within an enterprise.

BUILD TRUST—A VITAL COMPONENT OF ENDURING ACHIEVEMENT

I'm not upset that you lied to me, I'm upset that from now on I can't believe you.

—Friedrich Nietzsche

January 28, 1986, was that fateful day when the space shuttle *Challenger* broke apart 73 seconds into its flight, leading to the deaths of its seven crew members. The tragedy left a nasty scar on the US space program. Most of you have heard of this incident, but what we might be less familiar with the conclusions drawn by the Rogers Commission (appointed by President Ronald Reagan to investigate the catastrophe):

> *"NASA's organizational culture and decision making process were key contributing factors of the accident. Technicians, who were aware of problems, did not feel it was safe to bring it up due to low trust levels."*[1]

People can't do their best if they fear reprisals for raising issues that might be viewed as unpopular by their management or colleagues. As managers, we need to establish work settings in which personnel feel safe to do their best.

After all, organizations are comprised of people. Over time, people perform much better when they are relaxed and comfortable than when they are stressed and uncomfortable. In fact, performance often suffers in environments in which there is doubt, suspicion, and fear. Simply put, the time and energy spent looking over your shoulder diverts attention and effort away from the work at hand. For this reason, we as executives must fashion trust into the organizations that we lead.

Certainly, trust is good for business. High-trust work settings are efficient. All the focus is on results and not on each other. Work is done well, and quality is high in such environments. High trust businesses are resilient, as well. Trust provides strength against adversity within an enterprise. People just seem to pull together when they trust one another. Problems are addressed head-on—with no excuses made or expected. Work becomes play in high-trust companies. It is fun to see what can be accomplished when everyone works together to achieve a common goal.

To be sure, trust is a vital component of enduring achievement within an enterprise. That is why this topic has made *The Executive Checklist*:

Trust-building Checklist

✓ Model the Behavior
✓ Focus on the Outside
✓ Make It a "No Spin" Zone
✓ Don't Play Games
✓ Do Your Job
✓ Do Your Best
✓ Share the Wealth
✓ Keep It Light

Let us determine how best to build trust within a corporate culture by reviewing each item on the checklist.

CHECKLIST ITEM 1: MODEL THE BEHAVIOR

Trust starts at the top. People within an organization adopt the behaviors and attitudes of their leaders. If they see that their leadership team dodges conflict, makes excuses, and maneuvers around important issues, then they will think it's acceptable to be misleading and deceptive, too. On the other hand, if an executive is forthright, direct, and honest in his or her affairs, then staff members will exhibit those types of behaviors and will be trustworthy in their dealings.

Since the executive team sets the tone, it is imperative that he or she models the behavior that he or she wants to drive into the organization. It is will not suffice to say one thing and do another; that just leads to more deceitfulness across the enterprise. Rather, executives must strive to be a living example of decency in all that they do—this behavior results in a winning organization.

John Wooden, former University of California, Los Angeles (UCLA) men's basketball coach, comes to mind when considering the connection between leadership integrity and a winning team. Wooden's teams won seven consecutive National Collegiate Athletic Association (NCAA) championships—an astounding feat. He accomplished this by establishing trust and modeling the behaviors that he demanded from his players (for more, see *Wooden's Pyramid*).

See It in Action

Wooden's Pyramid

John Wooden was one of the most admired coaches in college basketball history. Adored by his players, Wooden was renowned for his short, simple, and inspiring messages to his players, many of which derived from what he called the "pyramid of success."

Driven by a need to redefine success and how to achieve it, Wooden developed his "pyramid for success" over a 14-year period. He completed his "Pyramid of Success" while a coach at Indiana State University in 1948, and used it as a coaching tool from then on.

His aim was to teach his players not only how to win on the basketball court but how to be successful in life. The pyramid consists of the following 15 elements:

✓ **Industriousness**—Great things come from hard work and careful planning;

✓ **Friendship**—Comes from mutual esteem, respect, and devotion;

✓ **Loyalty**—To all those who are dependent upon you;

✓ **Cooperation**—Help others and see the other side, too;

✓ **Enthusiasm**—Put your heart into all that you do;

✓ **Self-control**—Keep your emotions in check and use judgment and common sense;

✓ **Alertness**—Observe constantly and seek out opportunities to further the cause;

✓ **Initiative**—Develop the ability to make decisions and take action;

✓ **Intentness**—Stay the course and achieve your goal;

✓ **Condition**—Be physically and mentally ready for the challenge;

✓ **Skill**—Develop the fundamentals and be prepared to execute;

✓ **Team Spirit**—Put the team first;

✓ **Poise**—Be at ease under pressure;

✓ **Confidence**—Respect without fear comes with knowing that you're prepared;

✓ **Competitive Greatness**—Being at your best, when your best is needed.

As anyone can see, Wooden tied success not to achievement, wealth, or fame, but to how close a person came to his or her potential. By getting the absolute best out of his players, the coach led UCLA to ten NCAA championships.

There is clearly a correlation between a high-integrity team, like those that Wooden developed, and great success.

Sources:
1) *"John Wooden's Pyramid Stands Test of Time" by Robyn Norwood, Los Angeles Times, June 4, 2010;*
2) http://www.coachwooden.com/index2.html

However, success driven out of pronounced integrity isn't just for sports teams. Contemplate, for a moment, how an organization would fare in the marketplace if its personnel had a strong work ethic, always treated their customers fairly, and were enthusiastic about the work at hand. Chances are very good that that business would be booming and that its leader would have set a high standard for quality, honesty, and commitment to success, much like Wooden did with his basketball teams.

Thus, it is essential that executives be accountable for their actions, exhibit courage in the face of adversity, and be transparent—keeping no secrets—in their dealings with customers and colleagues, alike.

CHECKLIST ITEM 2: FOCUS ON THE OUTSIDE

An organization should always be focusing its energy on the outside—wowing prospects, servicing customers, and defeating the competition. Trust issues can arise when the people who belong to an organization lose that external focus. This can happen when personnel become distracted by internal conflicts that inhibit solid execution. Energy is sapped when they waste time on turf wars and other parochial in-house affairs. This is time that is not spent on winning business and overcoming rivals in the marketplace.

For this reason, executives must continually remind their organizations that the competition is outside, not inside, the four walls of the enterprise. We must remind our people that every moment we waste on infighting is another minute that our competitors are spending with our customers. Time spent on arbitrating disputes among departments is time lost on achieving the vision.

So, we must keep it simple, helping our organizations maintain their focus on the outside. We must promote a passion for the work that must be done to win the war that is being waged in the open market. After all, with passion come great products and amazing services—and we all know that outstanding products and service delivery find and retain customers while helping a business to grow.

CHECKLIST ITEM 3: MAKE IT A NO SPIN ZONE

Bill O'Reilly hosts *The O'Reilly Factor* on Fox News. The show is a platform for O'Reilly's own political points of view. In the program, he has a guest interview segment called the **No Spin Zone**, in which he claims that his visitors cannot spin their arguments for he will call them on it. And he does. At times it seems that his guests can't get a word in edgewise. Arguments between guests and host often break out. The show's contentiousness makes for good television.

Yet there is something for us as executives to gain from the concept of establishing an environment in which only facts are discussed and the truth is told. Seemingly, regardless of one's political leanings, we must create a No Spin Zone within the workplaces that we are charged with leading. It is merely a matter of good business to tell the truth and nothing but the truth.

Consider that consumer trust is at an all-time low. The international banking bust and the Great Recession of recent years contributed to the malaise, and the emergence of social media as a means of rapidly spreading the word about shady business practices and governmental corruption has only added fuel to the fire. One quickly gets the picture that it is in our best interests as senior leaders to build high-trust, transparent organizations (see *Trust: At a Ten-Year Low* for more details).

After all, spin is expensive. It simply costs more to spin the facts. Trust guru Stephen Covey explains it best in his book *Speed of Trust*:

> *"Instead of straight talk, much of organizational life is filled with spin. This creates what I call a 'spin tax' and is one of the main reasons why trust is low in so many organizations.... This diminishes trust and creates an additional 'withholding tax' where people withhold information and keep things close to the vest* [2]*."*

So, we must make our enterprises No Spin Zones—by insisting that problems be dealt with quickly, professionally, and most importantly, honestly. In this way we eliminate the costs of double- and triple-checking work and reduce the time and effort needed to spin the facts.

Indeed, by calling out "spin" behaviors (that only serve to propagate petty deceit and mistrust), a new tone can be set that permeates the entire organization. The new tone is one that promotes trust and focus on getting things done right the first time. It also encourages personnel to confront crises head-on without fear or derision within the ranks.

See It in Action

Trust: At a Ten-Year Low

Edelman is the world's largest public relations firm, with 66 offices and more than 4,500 employees worldwide. For the past 12 years, the firm has conducted the annual Edelman Trust Barometer Survey, which polls over 25,000 informed consumers from 25 countries on their trust of businesses and government entities. The results from the 2012 survey were quite revealing.

Trust in business has tumbled to a ten-year low.

The results pointed to lower levels of trust than those Edelman recorded following September 11, the dot-com implosion, and the collapse of AIG and Lehman Brothers. Clearly, we are at a trust deficit.

Here are some other interesting 2012 Trust Barometer findings:

✓ Nearly two-thirds of informed consumers (62 percent) trust corporations less than they did just one year ago.
✓ Only 17 percent said they trust information coming from a corporate CEO.
✓ Seventy-seven percent flatly refused to buy products or services from a company they distrusted.
✓ Seventy-two percent said they'd bad-mouth a distrusted company to a friend or colleague.
✓ By a 3-to-1 margin, consumers said government should intervene to regulate industries to restore public trust.

Surely, we can do better. If we don't, the implications of findings like the ones highlighted above will lead to business failure. With the emergence of social media, the sphere of influence spreads very quickly from the few to the many.

We as executives must heed this reality and strive to create organizations that are honest and trustworthy, or be prepared to handle the wrath of an angry customer base that can readily seek and find alternatives in which they can place trust.

Sources:
1) *Edelman Trust Barometer Annual Global Study 2012;*
2) *Corporate Mistrust: How Their Loss Is Your Gain by Harry Lew, National Ethics Association,* www.ethics.net, *June 27, 2012.*

CHECKLIST ITEM 4: DON'T PLAY GAMES

It is essential that executives model the behavior that we want to reinforce among our personnel. So don't play games with people and, just as important, don't allow games to be played by others on your watch. Instead, work to "keep it real" within the workplace by setting a clear direction, providing honest feedback, recognizing contributions, and celebrating completion.

Gamesmanship behavior presents itself in many different ways. Public admonishment of a subordinate by a supervisor, sharing office gossip about a teammate, sabotaging a colleague's work, taking credit for someone else's success, and various forms of one-upmanship among coworkers are all examples of games being played. Most of it is driven by an attempt by one staff member to outshine another in the hopes of being recognized as a superior talent worthy of reward or promotion. Don't allow this to happen in your organization. If you happen to witness such games being played, call people out on it.

By "keeping it real" and demanding the same of subordinates, you will create a work environment that is focused on delivering results and not one that is preoccupied by winning the silly games going on within the office. If you keep the emphasis on achieving the vision and reinforcing cooperation and candid interchange among colleagues, then office politics will diminish (for more insights on office politics, see *The Games People Play*).

See It in Action

The Games People Play

Robert Half, the professional staffing company, published the results from an office politics survey that they conducted in North America during summer 2012. Their findings were very interesting, pointing out that the games people play at work are as much a staple of the office setting as water coolers and laptops.

Here are some highlights of what they found:

✓ Sixty-two percent of respondents said office politics is somewhat or very necessary to advance one's career.

✓ Fifty-four percent of respondents said they either regularly participate in office politics or contribute to it when the issue is important to them.

✓ Fifty-four percent of respondents reported that gossiping and spreading rumors were the most common form of office politics in their organization.

✓ Thirty-nine percent of workers and twenty-seven percent of executives rated their work environments as very political.

The firm went on in its survey report to characterize the types of "game players" that are most prevalent in the workplace today. The top five are as follows:

✓ **The Gossip Hound.** This person loves spreading rumors and can often be found hovering around the water cooler, speculating about a variety of sensitive issues. Keep your distance from the Gossip Hound and don't say anything you wouldn't say to someone directly.

✓ **The Credit Thief.** This individual loves the spotlight and relishes taking credit for other people's work. When collaborating with a Credit Thief, document your contributions. Provide regular updates to your supervisor and correct any misrepresentations about your work.

✓ **The Sycophant.** "Shameless" is this person's middle name— he or she will offer lavish flattery to anyone who is in a position of power. Although it may be hard to watch, don't sweat the Sycophant's tactics. Most managers can see through them.

Give kudos to deserving individuals, regardless of their position.

✓ **The Saboteur.** Watch your back when working with this person, who loves to play the blame game and make others look bad. Limit your interaction with this master manipulator and make sure to stand up for yourself. Often, the Saboteur will back down when confronted.

✓ **The Adviser.** This professional is often closely aligned with an executive and serves as his or her eyes and ears. Develop a good rapport with the Adviser because he or she could have a direct line to the top.

Clearly, we have our work cut out for us in closing down games-manship at work and replacing it with straight talk and honesty. The time and effort spent playing games is time that is squandered, unable to be put to use moving an organization ahead.

Sources: "How to Navigate Office Politics: Your Guide to Getting Ahead" by Robert Half Staff, www.roberthalf.com, August 21, 2012.
"What Is the 'Hot' Topic in Office Politics?" by U.S. Daily Review Staff, www.usdailyreview.com, September 10, 2012.

CHECKLIST ITEM 5: DO YOUR JOB

Executive leadership can set an important tone within a corporate culture by regularly reinforcing a simple message to all personnel—"do your job." The implications of those three unassuming words abound. The following can easily be inferred from these words:

✓ staff members are duty-bound to focus their energy on doing their level best at their job assignments;

✓ workmates should direct all of their attention at performing their specific responsibilities and not be concerned with how others are carrying out their tasks;

✓ coworkers have to work together to deliver on their obligations to one
   another; and,

✓ colleagues must rely on others to do their jobs in order to be
   successful

If taken seriously and acted upon, each of these interpretations
of the message will strengthen behaviors that lead to trust within an
enterprise.

It is essential for us as leaders to make sure that our people understand their individual responsibilities and are accountable for delivering
on expectations. We cannot presume personnel will take charge if they do
not understand the job or recognize the desired results. Therefore, we must
be clear about what is to be done and what is to be delivered.

Once that understanding is established across the concern, we can
remind our staff members to, "do your job," which means working hard,
being prepared, paying attention to details, and putting the organization's
goals ahead of personal ones. When that happens, trust develops and
champions are made (see *The Patriots Way*, for an example of how having
a focus on doing your job can lead to winning championships).

See It in Action

The Patriots Way

There is a sign that is posted above the door as you enter the New
England Patriots locker room that reads Do Your Job. It was put there
at the direction of head coach Bill Belichick. It serves as a reminder to
his players to come to work each day ready to work and focus on doing
their jobs.

The words must have an effect. Since Belichick's arrival in New
England in 2000, the Patriots have become one of the most successful squads in National Football League (NFL) history. They have
won all but two American Football Conference East titles since
2001; have earned their way into the Super Bowl seven times (the

most by any team in the last 25 years); and have won the Super Bowl three times. It is an understatement to say that the team knows how to win.

Interestingly, on paper the team should not have accomplished as much as it has. Individual stats are generally lacking, and with an exception of a handful of players over the years, like future Hall of Fame quarterback Tom Brady, the Patriots have had few superstars on its roster.

Yet the franchise is a modern-day dynasty—and that doesn't just happen, especially in the era of parity (that is, League rules and practices are in place to ensure that all teams have roughly equivalent levels of talent) in the NFL. So what makes the Patriots different?

It begins with Belichick's clearly defining the responsibilities and expectations for every employee in the organization. It is impossible for a staff member to be accountable if they are unclear about duties and expected results. Belichick makes sure that everyone in the Patriots organization, from players and coaches to scouts and errand boys, understands what his job is and what he or she is expected to accomplish.

In this way, when the coach says, "Do Your Job," every member of the franchise knows what that means for his or her.

In the words of Tom Brady:

"Coach talks about doing your job and whatever your role may be.... You know that whenever your number is called you have to go out there and perform, because everyone on our team is counting on you. Starting quarterback or the left guard or the nickel defensive back, every job is important and when you are called upon to do that, the expectations are to go out there and play at a championship level, ... I think everybody who is active for this game understands the importance of their role and what they have to go out and do to be able to try to help us win."

Undoubtedly, placing emphasis on doing your job is one of the important ways in which trust is built and games are won.

Sources: *"Tom Brady Press Conference Transcript" posted by New England Patriots, www.patriots.com, January 18, 2013.*

CHECKLIST ITEM 6: DO YOUR BEST

It is our obligation as executives to establish an expectation among those in our organizations to always do their best. However, doing one's best does not mean having to be perfect. Rather, it is better to establish a work setting in which personnel strive to learn from mistakes and grow organizational knowledge through experience, than to create an environment that is so concerned with perfection that it stunts execution and stifles performance.

Trust is built in organizations that promote growth and learning. Removing the threat of reprisals when an error occurs serves to encourage risk-taking and problem-solving. Likewise, by investing in the development of the skills that personnel need to do their best, grows an organization's capabilities, resulting in a win-win for staff and firm alike. Such actions forge a confidence within employees that motivates them to give their all for the success of the enterprise.

It is personnel's commitment to "do your best" that separates elite organizations from the "also ran's." More high-quality work gets accomplished in less time, requiring fewer resources when everyone is determined to "do his or her best." Auspiciously, the more success that is achieved, the more trust that is established among members of an organization.

Familiarity may breed contempt, but winning breeds trust. An enterprise "wins" more, when everyone does his or her best.

CHECKLIST ITEM 7: SHARE THE WEALTH

Executives should be vigilant in both celebrating success and sharing in failure within their organizations. It builds trust and motivates staff when they recognize that their management team gives them credit when credit is due and takes responsibility when things don't work out the way that they were intended. There is not resentment or mistrust. The entire team feels like they are in it together when we as senior leaders "share the wealth."

However, sharing the wealth runs both ways. Everyone enjoys the successes. Personnel never tire of being recognized and celebrated for their accomplishments. However, disappointments need to be learned from and converted into motivating factors for the future. No one wants to be on a losing team, and too many gaffes can lead to long-term disaster for an enterprise. Therefore, it is we at the top of the organization who are accountable for acknowledging the victories and putting policies in place that help the members of the organization learn from the defeats.

Likewise, trust increases and performance improves in an organization in which the proceeds from the business are shared more equally between executives and staff. Several studies have found that wide gaps in pay between senior managers and personnel can negatively impact worker productivity, morale, and turnover. In 2010, a joint study by Northeastern University's business school and Bentley University found that employee productivity decreases as the disparity between CEO and worker pay increases.[3] It seems that great compensation inequalities serve to degrade the rank and file. There is simply no doubt that businesses do better in which the employees come first (see *Employees Come First at Whole Foods,* for a recent example).

It is in the best interests of all involved to share the wealth, both literally and figuratively—meaning, executives get recognized for developing great, high-trust organizations, workers respect and trust their leadership and get fairly compensated for their commitment to the cause, and shareholders gain from their investments in successful enterprises. Simply put, everybody wins.

See It in Action

Employees Come First at Whole Foods

At a recent Captains of Industry series interview with Bloomberg News, John Mackey, Whole Foods Market, Inc.'s Co-Chief Executive Officer said employees, not shareholders, need to be the first priority for businesses.

"*I really don't think shareholders should come first, I think it's fundamentally a bad strategy. . . . Happy team members result in happy customers; happy customers result in happy investors. If you put shareholders first, you won't get there.*"[4]

Mackey, 59, is an unconventional leader. For example, he has capped executive pay at 19 times the company's average hourly wage at Whole Foods—a marked difference compared to other firms like UnitedHealth Group, where the CEO-to-worker pay ratio is 1737:1.

It is not surprising that this self-proclaimed "conscious" capitalist has earned only $1 in salary and received no bonus in the past four years. Mackey believes that corporations have an obligation to share the wealth with employees and create value within the local communities in which a business thrives.

His approach is paying dividends. Sales at Whole Foods rose 16 percent to $11.7 billion in the fiscal year ended in September 2012, the third straight year with revenue growth of at least 12 percent. Shares have climbed more than fivefold since the grocer went public in 1992.

Not bad for a college dropout who cofounded a natural foods store in Austin, Texas, in 1978.

Sources: "*Whole Foods' Mackey Says Employees Should Come before Investors*," *by Brooke Sutherland, Bloomberg, January 18, 2013*.
http://www.payscale.com/ceo-income

CHECKLIST ITEM 8: KEEP IT LIGHT

It is important to establish a work setting that is comfortable for employees and conducive to getting things accomplished. Executives can promote more trust among contemporaries and coworkers when we keep it light and establish a positive atmosphere. People will work longer and harder when they like each other and feel a sense of togetherness.

We need to remove the drudgery and fear that can consume many workplaces. Workers in such settings do not trust each other and are not nearly as productive as workers in high-trust work environments, in which workers derive enjoyment from joint effort and coworkers share in collective achievement.

Recently, the research and analytics firm Gallup, Inc. conducted an innovative study on the causal effect of employee work setting perceptions on the bottom line and found that specific workplace conditions such as role clarity, feeling appreciated, coworker relationships, and opportunities to learn have an impact on organizational performance outcomes and a reciprocal relationship between employee satisfaction and financial performance[5]. These findings imply that happy workers make outstanding companies. So let's keep workers smiling.

After all, there is nothing wrong with making work fun. We all spend an inordinate amount of time working. Why not create a setting in which people can enjoy the effort and appreciate their cohorts? The model can certainly pay off. Most of the top firms listed in *Fortune Magazine*'s annual Best Places To Work edition showcase fun, employee engagement, and staff appreciation as hallmarks of their corporate cultures. Keeping it light makes a difference and promotes trust within the enterprise (see **Having Fun at DreamWorks Animation**, for an example from one of the regulars on *Fortune*'s list).

See It in Action

Having Fun at DreamWorks Animation

A regular top-20 company on *Fortune Magazine*'s **Top 100 Companies to Work For** list, the movie studio encourages its people to have "fun." For example, management brings fresh-juice trucks onto their campus to distribute free smoothies; employees are given stipends to personalize workstations, and last year, the crew held a Banana Splats party, at which staff members showed outtakes from a recent film.

The firm tries to keep it light to spark creativity and innovation. In fact, having fun is featured in the company's culture statement:

"At the heart of DreamWorks Animation is the desire to tell great stories and inspire audiences. The company's culture not only encourages employees to create but also to innovate and, ultimately, to have fun!"[6]

The "have fun" philosophy must be working. DreamWorks has attracted world-class creative talent and a strong and experienced management team, and developed advanced filmmaking technology and techniques that have contributed to the development of money-making franchise properties like Shrek, Kung Fu Panda, and Puss in Boots.

DreamWorks Animation serves as a fine example of a successful business that still has fun getting the job done.

Sources: *"Best Companies to Work for," Fortune, www.fortune.com, Jan. 17, 2013*
http://www.dreamworksanimation.com

IN CLOSING

It is up to us as executives and leaders to forge organizations that are steeped in trust and fortified by our commitment to create a workplace that enables people to get along and prosper. After all, no one wants to work with a jerk (see *Jerk Free at Plante & Moran*, for an example of what one firm has done to ensure a better work environment for its people).

Indeed, great things happen when people who work together trust each other. Consider these byproducts of high-trust work settings, for example:

- **Focus improves** – When trust is high, our focus and effort can remain on delivering superb products and services to our customers. Energy is conserved and saved for use on initiatives intended for competitive gain;
- **Rumors diminish**—When trust is high, there's no need to spread rumors or tell tales about colleagues. There is nothing to be gained by such behavior;
- **Success is celebrated**—When trust is high, a strong sense of team spirit develops. Everyone gets the chance to revel in the victories;
- **Infighting ends**—When trust is high, there's nothing to fight about. Accomplishments are recognized and credit is shared among those who worked to deliver the results;
- **Communication is enhanced**—When trust is high, communication becomes easier. No one is guarded or afraid to share information needed to get the job done;

- **Lessons are learned**– When trust is high, no one should be defensive. Personnel can readily learn from mistakes and move on;
- **Work becomes fun**—When trust is high, people enjoy their work and appreciate their coworkers;
- **Progress is made**—When trust is high, organizations simply perform better than those in which trust is lower;

By following the checklist for this chapter, we can cultivate all of these benefits and develop what is needed within our organizations to establish a foundation for enduring success. The benefits outlined above are certainly worth the effort.

In the next chapter, we will discover ways to build on our organization's newly founded trust and further engage our staff members in the process of defining and managing change.

Jerk Free at Plante & Moran

Plante & Moran is the nation's eleventh-largest certified public accounting and business advisory firm, providing clients with financial, human capital, operations improvement, strategic planning, technology selection and implementation, and family wealth management services. Plante & Moran has a staff of more than 2,000 professionals in 21 offices throughout Michigan; Ohio; Illinois; Monterrey, Mexico; Mumbai, India; and Shanghai, China.

The company also has a "jerk-free" policy published in its personnel manual.

Managing Partner Gordon Krater explains:

"The story goes that co-founder Frank Moran was adamant that the firm wouldn't hire or tolerate jerks," explains Krater. "When a staffer said that anyone can be a jerk at times, Frank countered by saying Plante & Moran was 'relatively jerk free.' The concept ended up memorialized in the personnel manual decades ago and remains there—and in our hiring practices—to this day." [7]

It looks as if the philosophy is working. Plante & Moran has the lowest employee turnover rate of any major accounting firm in the

United States, and its customer satisfaction is something to marvel at. Here are some highlights from the most recent surveys:

- Ninety-six percent say that they can depend on Plante & Moran to deliver on its promises;
- Ninety-five percent say that Plante & Moran puts clients' interests first;
- Ninety-two percent say Plante & Moran understands their industry / business;
- Ninety-six percent of clients rate Plante & Moran's performance as better than average, with more than one out of two rating Plante & Moran's performance as exceptional (60 percent);
- Seventy-five percent of clients say they have referred someone to Plante & Moran; and,
- Ninety-three percent say they are willing to be used as a reference

These results plainly indicate that Plante & Moran clients trust them. Surely, being "jerk free" has its benefits.

Sources: http://www.plantemoran.com/about/Pages/client-satisfaction.aspx

3

STRATEGY SETTING—TRANSLATING VISION INTO ACTION

Determine that the thing can and shall be done and then we shall find the way.

—Abraham Lincoln

Strategic planning is one of those things that every company claims to do, but few do it well. Many executives mistake annual budgeting for strategic planning. Because of this, countless organizations are ill-prepared for the competitive demands that lie ahead, and they lack the discipline and rigor needed to identify, organize, and execute the appropriate work in any sustainable way, leaving them to flounder in the New World economy that awaits us.

The following checklist is presented to assist in the recasting of strategic planning as an ongoing, continuous process used to identify, document, and oversee all of the strategic, tactical, and operational-related initiatives needed to revitalize the organization over time.

Strategy-setting Checklist

✓ Establish a New Ideology.
✓ Construct a Vision Story.
✓ Develop Business Principles.

✓ Create a Strategic Planning Program.

✓ Recognize the Implications of the Strategic Planning Process.

✓ Recognize the Implications of All Work Managed from a Strategic Plan.

✓ Build New Behaviors through Instituting Strategic Planning Practices.

✓ Don't Forget About Business Blind Spots.

Let's explore how each of these checklist items can reshape an organization's strategy-setting in the future.

CHECKLIST ITEM 1: ESTABLISH A NEW IDEOLOGY

In order to establish a new strategic platform for success, firms must embrace a new ideology for strategic thinking. There are forces at work in the early twenty-first century business world that are insisting that organizations embrace a new way of imagining the future. It includes concepts like

✓ establishing a sense of being "in it together" from within the organization because personnel who feel appreciated build superior products and provide outstanding service;

✓ viewing the enterprise from the outside-in as a means of better meeting the demands of an ever-discriminating customer base;

✓ enabling a work setting that promotes focus in a constantly changing business environment;

✓ cultivating a more independent and creative workforce that needs to be quicker on its feet than ever before in order to respond to the challenges that come with the new economy; and

✓ being better positioned to leverage the natural skills and manage the challenges that come with "Generation Y," the next wave of workers entering the job market.

To say that a paradigm shift of brilliant proportions is taking place within the business world today is an understatement. It is important to understand each of these points because they need to be incorporated into every organization's new ideology or vision for the future:

✓ **Be "In It Together"**— the old ways of running a company have given way to a new style of business management. The new style can be characterized as one in which "we're in it together." This new leadership paradigm calls for management to set direction and enable success. It welcomes rigor and discipline and encourages calculated risk-taking, as long as all of the issues are well understood and the actions to be taken are consistent with the direction in which senior leadership wants to take the enterprise. A strong sense of "togetherness" is also critical to overcoming adversity and tough times (see *Harry & David Are in It Together*, for an example of why this concept is so important in times of trouble).

See It in Action

Harry & David Are in It Together

In March 2011, Harry & David, one of the largest suppliers of premium fresh fruit and gourmet food gifts in North America, filed for Chapter 11. Its prenegotiated turnaround plan outlined a "back-to-basics" approach to returning the firm to profitability. The centerpiece of the strategy was dedicated to instituting an operational about-face.

The newly minted management team, brought in from Alvarez & Marsal (a company that specializes in performance improvement and interim management), quickly set the stage necessary to retune the ways and means of the company.

It took a committed workforce, one that felt like it was in it together with the leadership team, to make the essential changes. Within a few months Harry & David's product assortment was simplified, meticulous demand planning was instituted, operational efficiencies were gained, discount strategies were implemented, customer and gift experiences were enriched, and gross margins began to rise.

Less than six months after filing, in September 2011, Harry & David emerged from bankruptcy. The new and improved company had no long-term debt and had a strong foundation from which to grow. There is no doubt that its employees deserve the bulk of the credit. They pulled together when they needed to, and made it happen. In fact, many of the staff who were let go when the firm first spiraled out of control were rehired as the business regained its footing.

Harry & David continues to maintain a competitive advantage in the direct marketing gift space today because of its committed personnel being in it together.

Source: "*2012 TMA Annual Awards,*" Turnaround Management Association, November 9, 2012, p. 3.

✓ **Stay Focused**—It should be mentioned that superior companies seem to have the capacity to stay in the moment and remain focused even when bombarded by immeasurable distractions incessantly hurled from an ever-changing and dynamic business world. That's not to say that these firms don't make midcourse adjustments. To the contrary, the best run companies have a game plan that they are constantly monitoring and adjusting as new facts and details come to light during strategy execution.

✓ **Adopt Outside-In**—Today's executive teams have begun to place a needed emphasis on the service delivery aspects of the company. By doing so, we have come to realize that the best results are achieved by embracing an "outside-in" point of view—one that considers the impact of the organization's product and service offerings as well as its planned policy and procedural changes on the customer and other outside constituents before implementation. In this way, mistakes can be avoided and the need for rework minimized. For an example, see *Connecticut's Tax Department's Emphasis on Outside-In*.

See It in Action

Connecticut's Tax Department's Emphasis on Outside-In

A paradigm shift of brilliant proportions has taken place within Connecticut's Department of Revenue Services (DRS). The leadership team led by Commissioner Kevin Sullivan and his deputy, Joseph Mooney, has begun to place a needed emphasis on the service delivery aspects of the agency.

By doing so, DRS has come to realize that the best results are achieved by embracing an "outside-in" point of view—one that considers the impact of DRS policy and procedural changes on the taxpayer and other outside constituents before implementation. In this way, mistakes can be avoided and the need for rework minimized.

For years, the agency had been plagued with the bad press that comes on the heels of tax increases and the introduction of new tax policy. It was not unusual for changes in tax law to be implemented with not so much as an announcement to the taxpayer community. What is more, the language on new tax forms was often ill-conceived and confusing.

All of this led to great frustration among taxpayers and tax preparers within the state. Recognizing that people felt like they just were not being treated right, Sullivan decided that it was time to set a new direction—one that put the taxpayer first.

Highlights of the program include:

✓ creating and socializing a new vision for the agency;
✓ developing a Strategic Plan that supports the achievement of the vision;
✓ recasting his weekly senior leadership meeting into an executive steering committee for providing oversight on strategic initiatives;
✓ charging a plan administration office to oversee the execution of the strategic plan and its corresponding project portfolio management process;

✓ instituting biweekly project coordination meetings among those employees managing strategic projects within the agency: and

✓ provisioning necessary leadership, trust, team building, and project management training.

As a result, a "new normal" is being established at the tax department, one marked by efficient execution, taxpayer-friendly service delivery, and accurate and timely communication with the taxpayer community.

Some early results include:

✓ a new forms process aimed at simplifying the readability of agency forms and correspondence;

✓ a reorganized Operations Department and online taxpayer support function;

✓ a taxpayer community outreach program to solicit input from a cross-section of Connecticut state taxpayers: and

✓ increased use of online, television, and radio advertisements to raise awareness about new tax programs being instituted within the state.

Clearly, the agency's new ideology is taking hold, thanks to the commissioner's vision and commitment to change. We can expect more as these outside-in philosophies take hold and evolve across state government.

✓ **Cultivate Independence and Creativity**—Shifting gears to another topic, we all want to work in a gratifying and stimulating environment, one that brings out the best in our colleagues and us. But how do you cultivate such a work environment? The place to start is by building an independent and creative workforce.

Why? Independence among personnel equates to empowerment. An empowered workforce allows for better decisions to be made more quickly and closer to the action, and creativity spawns interest and excitement among staff members. Creativity leads to compelling product and service offerings; it serves to differentiate firms from their competition.

✓ **Prepare for Gen Y**—Meanwhile, in less than a decade from now, the Generation Y personnel will be firmly rooted within most large organizations around the world. As this continues, all kinds of enterprise-wide changes will likely result. From more fluid organizational design to location independence, this new wave of workers will influence strategic direction and business transformation. We are already witnessing a shift to social media-based business models as a result of Gen Y's effect on the marketplace. While the topic is further discussed in the next chapter, suffice to say that it is essential that any vision and strategic planning program include initiatives aimed at engaging the Gen Y workforce.

Indeed, all of the changing aspects of the business world described above play a role in how we must re-envision and reshape our organization's ideologies and strategic ambitions for tomorrow.

CHECKLIST ITEM 2: CONSTRUCT A VISION STORY

New ideologies are best articulated through a story about our organization's vision for the future. It is in our best interests to create exciting organizations that are substantially different from other companies in which they compete in order to attract and retain the best and brightest. This transformation starts with a vision so compelling and dramatic that the average working professional wants to be part of it. A vision statement doesn't cut it; a vision story does!

Above all else, a vision story must be engaging. People must be able to identify with what is being proffered within the story. They need to be able to see themselves working at that company. The story must be so riveting that a staff member will not be satisfied working at any other firm on the planet. Futuristic in its tone and loose and sinuous in its organization, a vision story is written as if the company has already completed the work needed to achieve its vision. Typically 15 to 20 pages in length, the story must be a vast and detailed discussion of what a company is to become in order to achieve its long-range goals.

Some organizations are willing to present the story in more elaborate ways, too. When working with the management team at the LexisNexis Insurance Software Division, for example, we developed the vision story as a series of related articles that were ultimately organized into a full-length magazine and distributed to each staff member via the US postal service. See *The LexisNexis Vision Magazine*, for more details.

Let a strong statement of the financial goal frame the vision story. People want to know the size of the company that they will be part of down the road. Thus the statement of financial goals will serve to inform their commitment and act as a differentiator among options (that is, small and growing, midsize and specialized, large and dominating, and so forth). It's important to people to identify with the size and goals of the firms for which they work.

However, the financial goal is just the beginning of the story. The rest of the tale must include details about the company, including such characteristics as:

- ✓ management style
- ✓ customer demographics
- ✓ growth strategies
- ✓ service delivery
- ✓ brand value
- ✓ operating model
- ✓ flexible workforce
- ✓ communication infrastructure
- ✓ diversity and inclusion

- ✓ leadership models
- ✓ product / service sets
- ✓ product distribution
- ✓ new business partnerships
- ✓ organizational structure
- ✓ process transformation
- ✓ performance metrics
- ✓ project portfolios
- ✓ governance frameworks

This is not to say that the vision story specifies what each of these characteristics is for the company. Each of the subjects on the list must be further refined and developed over the course of time that transpires between where an organization is today and where it ventures to go in the future.

Once the vision is defined, time must be dedicated to raising awareness of its content among staff and management alike. An entire employee engagement and Vision Socialization effort should quickly follow the publication of the story. As described in Chapter 1, town hall meetings, company pep rallies, and all-hands strategy off-site sessions are part of the socialization effort.

These activities must be done to help people better understand the vision and how they fit into the future of the organization. They also demonstrate the commitment of us, as executive leaders, to making the changes outlined in the Vision Story.

See It in Action

The LexisNexis Vision Magazine

A few years ago, it seemed as if LexisNexis Insurance Software division had lost its way. In response, the management team was looking for ways to re-establish the firm in the ultra-competitive world of property casualty software. Its first step towards revitalization was to build a new vision for the business.

Rather than using the same old tired techniques that had been used before—marked by gathering the senior leadership team at an off-site location to noodle out a one-paragraph vision statement (that described the firm as the best software business on the planet, or words to that effect) and later distributing the statement to all employees via email—the management team agreed to invest in developing a vision story that would engage staff and help them better understand where the company was heading.

Wanting a fresh new approach to the challenge, the management decided to present the vision story in the form of a magazine comprised of articles. Each article would be written by a member the senior leadership team. The magazine would be designed based on the *Harvard Business Review* format and style. It would be distributed to each staff member via the US postal service.

The reaction to the piece was exceptional. Staff members were pleasantly surprised to find a magazine focused on their company waiting in their mailboxes. Out of pure curiosity, most people read the magazine in one sitting. Soon after mailing copies of the publication, the management team followed up with a company-wide awareness session aimed at further assisting staff members in understanding the finer points brought out in each of the magazine articles (this awareness session is described further in *Let's Have a Vision Trade Show*, found in Chapter 1).

CHECKLIST ITEM 3: DEVELOP BUSINESS PRINCIPLES

As outlined above, a new ideology for strategic thinking is needed in order to establish a foundation for success within the New Normal. It follows that a new set of rules will be established in support of the new ideology. Business principles are those rules.

To be specific, business principles are nothing more than statements of executive management's predilection for how they prefer to run the business. Once in place, business principles become "Rules of the Road" for how personnel should plan, manage, and work within the organization. Together, the collection of business principles that a management team chooses to put in place provides an essential underpinning for the strategic agenda that will be used to reinvent the enterprise.

In most cases, no less that 12 and no more than 20 business principles are needed for an enterprise. Business principles can be categorized across three dimensions: people, process, and technology. After all, every business is comprised of people who do work using tools. It makes sense to have principles defined that address these universal aspects of an organization.

Here are some examples of the business principles that some of my clients have adopted:

Examples of People-Related Business Principles

✓ *A team-based management model will be adopted by the company to enhance the ability to better respond to emerging market opportunities.*

✓ *The business will aggressively leverage the emerging free-agent market.*

Examples of Process-related Business Principles

✓ *We will place an unrelenting focus on establishing a work environment that supports continuous transformation.*

✓ *Processes will be designed independently of current work locations and physical plant.*

Examples of Technology-related Business Principles

✓ *The information technology environment will be architected with resiliency and flawless integration in mind.*

✓ *With increasing business variability in mind, the work environment will be constantly monitored to identify opportunities to automate routine activities.*

When documenting business principles, it is essential that the rationale and implications for each one is provided. A principle's rationale is the "reason" why it is important that it be used within the enterprise, while its implications are the "price" an organization is willing to pay in order to realize its benefits.

See *Rebuilding Integrity Insurance*, for an example of a fully documented strategic business principle.

See It in Action

Rebuilding Integrity Insurance

A few years ago, Integrity Insurance wanted to recast the enterprise and break down the silos that were inhibiting efficient execution and performance. Julie Walker, vice president of strategic planning, decided that a new strategic planning program was needed, one that would drive change in the way work gets done.

We began by engaging the senior management team in the development of a set of business principles. The following business principle became one of the key drivers for the revitalization of the company, serving as a cornerstone for a company-wide re-engineering program:

Processes will be broadened to include all related responsibilities and tasks, free of existing organizational design or "chain of command."

Rationale:

Today, work within Integrity Insurance is delineated by business unit. Work is performed in one unit, and is then passed to the next for further piecework, much like an assembly line. This assembly line approach is becoming an unnecessary constraint. Its many hand-offs make it an expensive, time-consuming, and error-prone proposition.

The time has come for staff to assume the responsibility for getting the job done, regardless of position, organizational chart, or chain of command. The company's success in rebuilding the way work is done rests on defining business processes that have no organizational boundaries, and on preparing our personnel to "do whatever it takes" to get the job done.

Implications:

✓ Processes will need to be reviewed and redefined, independent of current organizational boundaries. Emphasis will need to be placed on performing the "whole job" instead of only specific pieces. Artificial boundaries that promote a "silo" mentality need to be eliminated.

✓ Jobs will be redefined. All attendant responsibilities and commitments related to performing the "whole job" will need to be folded into job specifications.

✓ Managers will need education on how to manage the process to optimize results rather than managing the activities of people performing the work.

✓ The re-engineering of business processes will be necessary to ensure that "best practices" and other quality standards are designed into new processes.

✓ Training is a must. Specifically, educating employees about new organization designs, process definition, and job responsibilities is essential in gaining buy-in and reducing feelings of friction or alienation that often come with change.

CHECKLIST ITEM 4: CREATE A STRATEGIC PLANNING PROGRAM

It's very easy to get distracted if your strategic plan lacks clarity or detail, or exists only in one's head. Too many clients tell me that they have a strategic plan, but they are unable to produce it when asked to provide me with a copy for review. What they often give me are expense estimates, revenue forecasts, and margin targets. Well, that is not a strategic plan—that's an annual budget!

When such is the case, it's time to establish a Strategic Planning Program that will create the initial strategic plan and introduce a continuous process for maintaining it over the course of time.

Here's a proven, four-step process for establishing a strategic planning programs:

1. Establish a baseline.
2. Compare the baseline to the vision.
3. Create a strategic plan that bridges the gaps.
4. Institute a plan administration process.

It has been used with all kinds of clients, from the US Marine Corps to The Home Depot.

The first step towards establishing a strategic planning program involves the creation of a baseline. A baseline defines the current state of the business. It characterizes the enterprise across the very dimensions outlined in the organization's vision (see above), including: product and service offerings, pricing, distribution, and customer support. It also characterizes the internal people, process, and technology used to deliver value to the organization's stakeholder community.

It's important that this baseline mirror reality. Therefore, the baseline report must reflect the organization, with all of its warts and blemishes. Without this understanding, it's possible that important improvement areas will be missed and that the work that is necessary to address these shortcomings will not be reflected in the strategic plan—potentially sabotaging the organization's ability to achieve its vision.

With a baseline assessment in place, the next step in establishing a strategic planning program is to compare the baseline to the entity's vision for the future. This comparison is essential because it will determine the gaps that exist between where the firm is today and where it is heading in the future. Each gap that is identified is then translated into a project or program to be included in the strategic plan.

A strategic plan that charts how the firm will get from its current state to the achievement of its strategic vision is developed in the next step. By definition, the strategic plan is comprised of a set of well-documented projects and programs that bridge the gap between baseline and target. These initiatives are spread across a multi-year timeline and include a full understanding of interdependencies, completion criteria, and detailed execution task lists for each initiative. Without this detail, you don't have a strategic plan, just a vague itinerary (one that can easily be abandoned if a new thought comes around).

The final step in establishing a strategic planning program is the creation of a strategic plan administration process. This allows firms to make appropriate midcourse adjustments. Plan administration work involves the coordination, review, and resetting/reconfirmation of the firm's projects and programs. In effect the strategic planning process is responsible for ensuring

✓ executive management review and ownership of the strategic plan;

✓ the existence of an effective means for the business to articulate new strategic initiatives;

✓ the "spearheading" of appropriate changes to existing strategic project/ programs plans; and

✓ the proper prioritization of newly defined and sanctioned work efforts.

In essence the strategic plan administration process allows for the strategic plan to be refined and updated as the firm evolves over time. Clearly, it is no small task to institutionalize plan administration within an enterprise. However, it is the very institutionalization of the process that is necessary to ensure that companies stay the course in pursuit of their strategic visions.

CHECKLIST ITEM 5: RECOGNIZE IMPLICATIONS OF STRATEGIC PLANNING PROGRAM

The installation of a strategic planning program becomes an important means of turning the widely accepted and outdated idea about strategic planning as being nothing more than an annual budget planning exercise on its ear.

It calls for strategic planning to become a constant, continuous process that ensures that businesses are able to adjust and evolve as competitive necessities dictate. In fact, when the program is fully realized, all the work of the organization is accounted for and included in the strategic plan forevermore.

By embracing this notion, the organization begins to clearly distinguish the value of the strategic planning discipline as a means for evaluating future business options and investment choices. By properly documenting the plan, the enterprise has an "organizational memory" that can be referenced in the future by the next generation of leaders.

There are many implications of putting such a program in place. For instance, we should consider:

✓ the strategic planning process must be documented and published;
✓ personnel (at all levels) must be trained in the planning process and be required to apply it in all that they do;
✓ the strategic planning program must include a means for nominating new projects and programs for consideration by the executive team;

✓ a strategic planning office must be staffed in order to administer the planning process and ensure its integrity; and

✓ the management team must be prepared for some resistance among their ranks and be willing to work to keep each other honest as the new planning behaviors are being learned.

CHECKLIST ITEM 6: RECOGNIZE IMPLICATIONS OF ALL WORK MANAGED FROM A STRATEGIC PLAN

An enterprise should ensure that all of its work (and related workload) is accounted for within its strategic plan. This is so because everyone must be able to discern any unintended organizational conflicts that may result in the pursuit of a new strategic idea prior to staffing and funding it.

There are many implications of managing an enterprise in this way, including:

✓ current staff load must be understood and mechanisms put into place to better understand ramifications of alternative staffing scenarios;

✓ provisions must be incorporated into the process that ensures executive steering committee participation in project selection and priority-setting;

✓ a communications program must be put in place to ensure that all staff fully understand shifts in staffing that are needed to pursue new strategic initiatives;

✓ organizational elements, like weekly project coordination meetings and project reviews, must be put into place to ensure that a project work is properly harmonized within the company; and

✓ The ever-changing strategic plan must be communicated regularly throughout the enterprise.

Refer to *Insurity's Strategic Staffing Model*, for more on how one insurance software firm put this concept into place.

See It in Action

Insurity's Strategic Staffing Model

Insurity delivers policy administration systems for use by Property & Casualty Insurance carriers. The business has grown substantially since its founder and current CEO, Jeffrey Glazer, started the company nearly 30 years ago. A true original, Glazer is an industry thought leader with a rich history of trailblazing innovative ways to leverage technology to better position insurance companies for the future. It's no wonder that Insurity was one of the first companies to grasp the significance of managing all work as a portfolio of projects within a strategic plan.

Last year, I worked with the Insurity management team to take the concept one step further. Together, we reconfigured the staffing model so that it is better aligned with the firm's strategic project portfolio.

In this way, the company's resources are organized to provide better products and services to its ever-more sophisticated and discriminating customer base. The staffing model shifts as new projects and initiatives are added to the portfolio. Company-wide improvement initiatives are spearheaded into the organization via a highly specialized, shared services group designated to manage a portfolio of projects aimed at establishing best practices within the firm.

The approach is already paying dividends as customer satisfaction measurements are showing significant improvements and industry analysts continue to give Insurity's products high marks. It serves as a good example of the new breed of strategic thinking in action.

CHECKLIST ITEM 7: BUILD NEW BEHAVIORS THROUGH INSTITUTING STRATEGIC PLANNING PRACTICES

One can safely assert that good things result when a strategic planning process becomes a foundation stone for the enterprise. All kinds of new behaviors are forged as planning becomes a continuous activity and strategic thinking becomes a natural tendency that brings about more order and control, and less confusion and waste.

Here is just a sampling of some of the new behaviors that result as new ways of thinking and doing become institutionalized through strategic planning:

- ✓ Because the planning program encourages everyone in the organization to contribute ideas for new initiatives *more inclusive behavior* becomes woven into the culture.
- ✓ In time, work becomes more deliberate and better organized. Consequently, an air of discipline falls about the enterprise, and staff naturally behave in a *more disciplined* manner as they go about their daily activities.
- ✓ The typical insularism that has become common among many of today's leaders is moderated because the new planning approach requires senior executives to adopt a *more participatory management style* in order to be effective. They learn to keep each other honest as they come together to plan and develop strategy.
- ✓ The emphasis on project management as a means to run strategic initiatives and manage work leads to better teamwork. This newfound *cooperative behavior* pays big dividends to the enterprise.

CHECKLIST ITEM 8: DON'T FORGET ABOUT BUSINESS BLIND SPOTS

There is a scientific principle known as the theory of incongruency. It suggests that our expectations cloud our perception. If we don't expect to see something, we simply will not see it. Stated another way, we see what we expect to see. The theory suggests that the rest, or what we do not see, falls prey to a virtual blind spot created by our brains when something appears that is not expected.

Strategic planning work is susceptible to this same type of blind spot. Many breakthrough ideas are ignored or dismissed because business leaders are unable to see the value of a new idea that doesn't fit within their current expectations of what will work within their firm or industry (see *Blind Spot Sideswipes Swiss Watchmaking Industry*).

Senior leaders must avoid falling prey to this type of blind spot. The best way to do that is to expand our awareness of all of the possibilities, extend our thinking through new experiences. In other words, we need to be deliberate about getting out of our comfort zones.

Here are some ideas for pushing ourselves (and our organizations) out of the comfort zone:

- ✓ **Leave Your Stripes at the Door**—create opportunities to discuss "big ideas" with subordinates and listen carefully to their ideas. Don't dismiss something that sounds silly, as this may be the theory on incongruency kicking in.
- ✓ **De-emphasize the Hierarchy**—break tradition when in the process of problem-solving on broad organizational issues; skip a level down into the organization and gain new perspectives. Just be sure to let your management team know that you're going to be doing it, so that they don't overreact.
- ✓ **Confront Fear**—if you witness behavior that may be construed as posturing among your management team, call them on it. Discuss the behavior, trying to get at the underlying cause. It could be that an unfounded fear or concern is stifling breakthrough thinking.
- ✓ **Discourage Groupthink**—instead, promote speaking for oneself. Whenever you hear someone on your management team begin a sentence with something like, "I think we all believe…," it is quite possible that the team has fallen into some form of groupthink. Squelch it immediately. Ask your staff member to speak for just him- or herself. In this way, you're encouraging others to express their opinions, too. This establishes an environment in which topics can be debated and counterviews can be expressed without fear of reprisal.
- ✓ **Encourage Diversity and Inclusion**—people at different levels of status, with different skills, styles, and backgrounds, can all earn the right to participate, influence, decide, lead, and succeed. Include different people with diverse backgrounds and experiences in the discussion. You may be surprised at the outcome.
- ✓ **Create Recognition Opportunities**—sometimes terrific opportunities (think Swiss watchmakers) are repressed by a corporate culture that

has demonstrated that it is not open to new ideas. By establishing mechanisms that foster ways for individuals or work units to be recognized for "out-of-the-box" thinking, a leader can begin to change the very culture that has inadvertently muted the growth potential of a business.

✓ **Just Shake It Up**—force the organization out of its comfort zone by doing things that break tradition. Bring a boom box to your next quarterly staff meeting and play some upbeat music while your people are gathering. Host a question-and-answer session with subordinates and toss a candy to a person who asks a good question or raises an important issue. Do something that shakes up the norm.

By seeking out ways to shake things up, both personally and professionally, we can create an environment that enables the kind of thinking and problem-solving needed to identify the next "big thing."

See It in Action

Blind Spot Sideswipes Swiss Watchmaking Industry

There's a classic example of an industry-wide blind spot in action that comes from the Swiss watchmaking industry. It truly had a devastating impact.

Did you know that the Swiss invented quartz movement watches? Indeed, the technology came out of one of the Swiss watch industry labs, but was quickly disregarded by industry thought leaders because they considered the quality of the quartz design inferior to their century-old way of doing things.

Seeing the potential while visiting a widely attended industry trade show, the Seiko watch company of Japan adopted the quartz technology to fill the demand for inexpensive watches, and within ten years, the Swiss watchmaker's market share fell from 65 percent to below 10 percent.

Sadly, it is estimated that as many as fifty thousand Swiss watchmakers lost their jobs because of the blind spot.

TO CLOSE

With the speed of change and velocity at which information comes hurtling at us, it will be very easy for today's executive teams to get distracted. Without a good plan and the processes needed to support its evolution, there will be a tendency to blindly chase any idea that holds promise—even if pursuing a distraction causes businesses to lose ground and fritter away precious assets in the process.

It is hoped that, with a better understanding of the eight items that comprise this Strategy Setting Checklist, an executive leader will be better positioned to help his or her organization institute a rock-solid strategic planning practice, one that will separate it from the "also-ran's."

4

ENGAGE STAFF—THE WAY TO GAIN SUPPORT AND ACCELERATE SUCCESS

We become what we behold.

—William Blake

Having articulated the strategic direction, we turn to the next item on the *Executive Checklist*, which involves the process of engaging staff in the transformation effort required to achieve the company's vision. We cannot renovate the enterprise without buy-in and commitment from the people doing the work. So, once we establish ourselves as leaders who can be trusted, we must set our sights on engaging our personnel in the change management effort required to realign our organizational structures, refurbish our product and service delivery models, and renovate our enterprises for continued success in the early twenty-first century.

This may not be easy. Workforce dynamics are radically changing in ways that we have never witnessed in the past. The situation can be best characterized as a melding of the old and the new. Older personnel are extending their careers because of the financial pressures brought about by shrinking retirement savings and the systematic dissolution of employer-sponsored pension plans.

This trend is coupled with the fact that the next generation of younger workers is entering the workplace with a new set of assumptions about how work is to be done, and is subsequently insisting that significant changes be made in exchange for their commitment and loyalty. Together, these developments are shaking the foundation of today's organization—and deepening the challenges related to employee engagement as it relates to reimagining the possibilities for tomorrow's business entities.

The checklist provided below outlines the important elements of staff engagement:

> **Staff Engagement Checklist**
>
> ✓ Decide to engage.
> ✓ Promote the new culture.
> ✓ Inspire early adopters.
> ✓ Plan for Generation Y.
> ✓ Include inclusion.
> ✓ Tie engagement to measurement and reward programs.

This checklist is intended to be referenced as we, as executive leaders, go about the important work of gaining the necessary employee support to accelerate successful transformation. Let's take a closer look at each of the items on the list.

CHECKLIST ITEM 1: DECIDE TO ENGAGE

Executives must place a value on, and be deliberate in, their efforts to engage personnel in the change management process. If you do not shine a lens on the process of engagement and make it a priority, it will likely not happen.

Some management teams that I've worked with over the years often give short shrift to the importance of being purposeful in staff engagement. Many managers adopt the attitude *"Just tell them what to do . . . they don't have to like it."* However, that approach simply does not work. We just can't expect people to do what they don't understand. Therefore, we must engage and be resolute in formalizing a dedicated program to do so.

The engagement program is continuous by nature and consists of the following elements:

- ✓ **Executive Sponsorship:** As senior leadership, we must own the engagement program and ensure its ongoing success. It is our behavior that others will model. By demonstrating our commitment to the program, we instill its value in our mid-tier and supervisory-level managers. We gain more momentum with staff when middle and operational managers make staff engagement a priority as well.

- ✓ **Engagement Strategy:** The methods, tactics, and processes intended to be employed at any given time in order to engage staff in change management are the centerpiece of the engagement program. Of course, the elements described in this chapter should be accounted for in the strategy. However, the details related to how those elements should be implemented depend on the specific underlying forces present within a particular organization. Nonetheless, having an effective plan and maintaining it over time is the key to success in staff engagement.

- ✓ **Communication Framework:** It is important for executive management to continually communicate the strategy and vision that underpin an organization's transformation. The type of messaging that management uses will shift over time relative to where an enterprise is in the execution of its strategies. Hence, a communication framework is a necessary component of an engagement program—it ensures that we deliver the "right" message at the "right" time.

  For example, when a new strategy is launched, initial messaging should be aimed at stimulating staff understanding of the new approach. As staff members begin to take action in support of the new initiative, messaging then shifts away from awareness to providing meaning for the work at hand. Once personnel start to gain meaning from their work, they develop passion for what they are accomplishing. It is here that our communication effort evolves, yet again, to one that encourages curiosity about what comes next. Engagement is achieved when staff begins to strive to go above and beyond for the sake of the enterprise.

✓ **Program Administration:** While it is true that the engagement strategy is the centerpiece of the program, those strategies must evolve over time in order to remain fresh and relevant. Therefore, it is imperative that a program administration function be established to maintain the program and ensure its uninterrupted advancement.

By placing emphasis on engagement and driving an official program with the types of mechanisms described above, we can expect the following results:

✓ **Enhanced Workplace Profile**: as the old adage suggests, *"you get more flies with honey than with vinegar."* Attractive workplaces attract good workers. A highly engaged workforce is very attractive to potential employees. If your staff creates a buzz in the marketplace because of its engagement, your organization will never want for qualified candidates to satisfy its employment needs;

✓ **Better Operational Decision-making**: stronger engagement brings improved operational decision-making and front-line leadership to an organization. Staff members are more willing to rise to the occasion when working for an organization that they believe in. Indeed, new and diverse solutions are more readily brought to the fore within enterprises that have committed personnel.

✓ **Improved Performance**: a work setting that seeks engagement and provides opportunities for staff to be heard and feel valued will perform better than one that fails to recognize the importance of employee buy-in and understanding. It is through greater engagement that better understanding of the "big picture" is achieved. When staff know where the organization is heading

and how they fit into the vision for the future, they are better
positioned to introduce new ways of thinking and doing—
improving the long-term performance of an organization (see
Zappos: The Poster Child of Employee Engagement, for an example
of how this online retailer remains so successful even in today's
slower economic times);

✓ **Broader Market Reach**: an engaged workforce supercharges the reach
of any organization. Staff member commitment and enthusiasm is
contagious. Customers flock to enterprises where the employees reflect
a strong desire to satisfy their needs and wishes.

Better results, a stronger workforce, and broader market reach make
a very compelling business case for implementing a formal engagement
program. However, the program plan must account for some of the subtleties that come with the next generation of employee of whom we must
engage.

See It in Action

Zappos: The Poster Child of Employee Engagement

Zappos, the online shoe and clothing retailer based out of Hender-
son, Nevada, is the poster child for employee engagement. Its 1,500
employees support an operation that generates an astounding $7 mil-
lion per day in sales. Its unique culture serves to engage a committed workforce and, ultimately, contributes to the firm's incredible
success.

The executive team wants to ensure that every new hire will
immediately contribute to the firm's over-the-top customer service
ethos. Thus, it has instituted a highly extensive interview process to
safeguard fit. Only 1 in 100 applicants is awarded a job at Zappos.
If you want to work there, your passion must shine through when
interviewing.

Once an applicant is successfully through the gauntlet, the message
becomes very clear, *"Buy into what we are doing here or we will pay you*

to leave." The company has a policy that will pay a new hire $2,000 to resign if the person finds that he or she can't quickly assimilate into the company's vibrant culture. It is an understatement to say that engagement is important at Zappos.

The firm's annually published *Culture Book* is a great example of the importance that has been placed on employee buy-in of the corporate philosophy. It is exclusively developed and produced by staff members. The book contains a variety of contributions from personnel exemplifying what it means to work at the online retailer. Its photos and short stories all serve to reinforce Zappos's cultural norms and values.

Recently, the company has even created a spin-off venture called Zappos Insight, a management consulting and training business that provides employee engagement and service delivery offerings to organizations interested in soliciting ideas about the way in which Zappos built its business. Attendance at one of its regularly scheduled three-day seminars runs $6,000.00 per person. But it may be worth the price of admission to gain the staff engagement needed to reinvent an organization.

Nonetheless, Zappos is a new economy enterprise that has figured out a way to engross and inspire its staff. Its success, even in the face of a downtrodden economy, indicates that the company is onto something that every executive should become aware of and better understand.

Source: "*Zappos Hits the Jackpot with Employee Engagement in Las Vegas,*" by Marc Wright, http://www.simply-communicate.com/case-studies, November 29, 2010.

CHECKLIST ITEM 2: PROMOTE THE NEW CULTURE

Every organization that embraces change and transformation has an opportunity to cultivate something that is original and exciting. Marketing the new culture is a vital means of building and maintaining a remarkably talented labor force. Accordingly, outreach and promotion are essential elements of staff engagement.

In fact, it behooves an organization to market its vision and its culture to both current and prospective employees. By doing so, we not only help our personnel understand what we are attempting to create over time, but we are also starting the process of the engagement of potential staff members by promoting our new culture in the marketplace (see **Google Sells Itself**, for an example of what the Internet juggernaut is doing to promote its culture).

See It in Action

Google Sells Itself

Google has grown by leaps and bounds since its founding in 1998. Besides serving up a plethora of web-based tools that have made life easier for individuals and businesses to navigate and leverage the power of the Web, the company has attracted some of the best minds in the world to come and work there.

Part of the attraction is Google's unique culture, which it promotes readily as a means of setting it apart from other Silicon Valley businesses. Here's how the firm describes its culture:

"It's really the people that make Google the kind of company it is. We hire people who are smart and determined, and we favor ability over experience. Although Googlers share common goals and visions for the company, we hail from all walks of life and speak dozens of languages, reflecting the global audience that we serve. And when not at work, Googlers pursue interests ranging from cycling to beekeeping, from frisbee to foxtrot.

We strive to maintain the open culture often associated with startups, in which everyone is a hands-on contributor and feels comfortable sharing ideas and opinions. In our weekly all-hands ("TGIF") meetings—not to mention over email or in the cafe—Googlers ask questions directly to Larry, Sergey and other execs about any number of company issues. Our offices and cafes are designed to encourage interactions between Googlers within and across teams, and to spark conversation about work as well as play."

These statements ooze of employee engagement. From its commentary on cultural diversity and inclusion to its description of easy executive access, Google sells itself to its staff and would-be personnel. Shoot, it makes me want to be a "Googler," too!

Source: *http://www.google.com/about/company/facts/culture/*

There are all sorts of ways to convey information about the new culture under development. Here are just a few ideas that can be used to promote and inform:

✓ Use popular **social media** sites like Twitter and Facebook to excite potential new hires.
✓ Design **web-based promotional campaigns** on job boards or professional social media sites like LinkedIn.
✓ Present **pop-up messages** on company email sites that contain important news about happenings within the enterprise.
✓ Develop and publish **executive blogs** on the organization's intranet that serve to raise awareness and educate in-house staff on new initiatives.
✓ Craft and **publicize incentive programs** that promote engagement.
✓ Build **on-boarding practices** that deeply immerse new hires into the culture and norms of the enterprise.

Regardless of the media used, the messaging must be consistent and on-point—appealing and informative to both internal and external audiences. In this way, we will be sure to engage current and aspiring staff members in the organization's change manifesto.

CHECKLIST ITEM 3: INSPIRE EARLY ADOPTERS

As already mentioned earlier in the chapter, executives must ensure that the organization's vision, and the major strategies by which it will be achieved, are collaboratively developed and understood by all. There will be a subset of staff members who quickly embrace the proposed changes and will wholeheartedly volunteer to assist in making them happen.

It is these "early adopters" whom we must inspire. They are the ones who will help the leadership team further socialize goals, operationalize strategies, and engage other employees in acceptance of the corporate vision and associated transformation program. The early adopters are the ones who will be chosen to manage initial change initiatives, facilitate focus groups, and serve on project teams (for an example, see *Employees Lead the Charge at Molex*).

When suitably stimulated, the early adopters can become the human manifestation of change. Executives need to recognize the possibilities and enthusiastically encourage employees to exercise self-initiative within each person's own sphere of influence and take on the challenges that he or she recognizes as being inhibitors to organizational revitalization.

By so doing, a grass-roots transformation movement will begin to effect change from the bottom up. When that type of employee-driven movement takes root, it can be much more powerful and influential than any top-down, executive engagement effort ever can. All thanks to motivated, early adopters.

Of course, nothing like this happens by accident. Formal, deliberate action is necessary to engage and inspire those personnel who are eager to change and willing to go above and beyond to assist in changing the culture. This is one of the best ways in which we can drive desired results within our organizations.

See It in Action

Employees Lead the Charge at Molex

Molex is one of the largest manufacturers of electronic components in the world. The company operates 40 manufacturing locations in 16 countries and employs over 34,000 people. Its portfolio is among the most extensive in the industry, with over 100,000 products, including everything from electronic, electrical, and fiber optic interconnects to switches and application tooling. Its customers include telecom, computer, automotive, and medical equipment companies, as well as military markets around the globe.

Headquartered in Lisle, Illinois, the firm has a huge global presence. More than 60 percent of its revenue is generated by its Asia Pacific region. It generated nearly $3.5 billion in revenue in 2012. Its business vision is to become a $5 billion business by 2015.

As an early enablement measure, the executive leadership team kicked off a full-blown employee engagement program last year within its Asia Pacific region. The effort spanned 7 countries and touched over 10,000 employees. Driven by the results from a recent staff member survey, the centerpiece of the program is employee-led focus groups intended to garner more comprehensive staff involvement in the necessary change management process.

More than 500 staff members participated in over 50 focus groups. Each focus group was facilitated by one of the firm's employees from within the local operation. These early adopters led their focus group colleagues through discussions on survey findings, all in an effort to determine recommendations for change.

Once the results of each focus group were packaged, local leadership teams reviewed and validated each action plan, determining how best to implement the group's recommendations within their areas of responsibility. Molex's senior management, including Martin Slark, CEO, and Ana Rodriguez, global senior vice president of HR, took that work and began to socialize it through town hall meetings with employees of each operation effected.

It's still too early in the execution of the ideas created within the focus groups to determine the long-term improvements that will result. However, it is certain that Molex's change effort is greatly enhanced by gaining the support of, and leveraging, its early adopters in the company's transformation program. Stirring workers to take on the responsibility of engaging their cohorts in planning for necessary changes is a sure-fire way to gain support and momentum.

Sources:
1) *"Interconnecting the Globe: Molex Focuses on Employee Engagement in Asia Pacific South," Towers Watson, http://www.towerswatson.com/newsletters/ strategy-at-work/9022, February 2013 ;*
2) http://www.molex.com/molex/index.jsp

CHECKLIST ITEM 4: PLAN FOR GENERATION Y

From an early age, they were told that they were the best, were awarded trophies just for showing up, and were groomed by overly involved parents who hovered like helicopters around them monitoring their every move. Generation Y (or Gen Y, for short) includes those individuals born between the years 1980 and 2000. Also known as "the Millennials," this generation of worker is bringing with it a myriad of expectations and demands that must be understood in order to suitably engage them in the organizational transformation efforts that we, as today's leaders, are responsible for implementing.

Here is a snapshot of the Gen Y worker:

✓ technologically savvy;

✓ continuously multitasks;

✓ impersonal communicators;

✓ in quest of constant feedback;

✓ driven by immediate gratification;

✓ exceedingly abrupt;

✓ information hungry;

✓ short of attention;

✓ desires group acceptance;

✓ needs high degree of praise;

✓ searches for personal understanding;

✓ stressed-out (see *Stressed Out in America*)

See It in Action

Stressed Out in America

Since 2007, the American Psychological Association commissioned an annual nationwide survey as part of its Mind/Body Health campaign to examine the state of stress across the country and understand its impact. The **Stress in America**™ survey measures attitudes and perceptions of stress among the general public.

According to the most recent survey, Generation Y is the most stressed-out generation in America.

Here are some of the highlights from the study:

✓ Work is a substantial stressor for 76 percent of Millennials.

✓ Younger Americans report experiencing the most stress and the least relief. They report higher stress levels than older generations and say they are not managing it well.

✓ Each generation experiences negative consequences of stress, but Millennials are most likely to say that they engage in unhealthy behaviors because of stress and experience symptoms of stress.

✓ More than 52 percent of Millennials report having lain awake at night in the past month due to stress, compared to 48 percent of Gen Xers, 37 percent of Boomers, and 25 percent of Matures.

✓ Additionally, 44 percent of Millennials report experiencing irritability or anger due to stress, compared to 36 percent of Boomers and 15 percent of Matures.

✓ Millennials and Gen Xers are most likely to say that they are stressed by work, money, and job stability, while Boomers and Matures are more likely to be concerned with health issues affecting their families and themselves.

While most Americans are experiencing some uptick in stress, likely due to the recent economic times, it is interesting that Gen Y is taking it the worst. It seems that it has been difficult for them to come to grips with the fact that their expectations of "life after school and parents" are proving to be unrealistic when confronted with the harsh realities awaiting them once they are out on their own.

This is an important trend for executives to monitor because of the implications that it has for the future staffing, training, and health benefits needs of American organizations.

Source: "Stress in America™: Missing the Health Care Connection," American Psychological Association, http://www.apa.org/news/press/releases/stress/index.aspx, February 7, 2013.

The Gen Y worker is difficult to engage and is not easily managed through conventional means because quality of life is more important to him or her than titles and compensation packages. As a result, we will have to carefully contemplate how best to pique their interest and participation in organizational change processes. Here are some ideas worth considering[1]:

1. **Redefine Titles**—Since Gen Y workers demand collaboration and flexibility, positions and job titles may need to be redefined or removed altogether, if existing titles hinder teamwork and prevent required organizational elasticity;

2. **Harness Social Media**—The Gen Y workforce will continue to call for more sophisticated means of "staying connected." Therefore, we must make the utilization of social media a priority item to be strategized and instituted within the enterprise immediately;

3. **Enable a Free Agent Market**—Millenials want to be free agents. Therefore, provisions must be made to ensure that free agent personnel are trained in the organization's operating policies, procedures, and quality standards, so that they can assimilate quickly and deliver the desired results;

4. **Promote Location Independence**—Given the need for workforce (and, therefore, operational) fluidity, physical location independence will be a compulsory part of business as well. Plans to establish remote work locations that can be staffed on-demand by a team assembled of free agents will likely be part of the near-future business landscape.

5. **Provide "Lifestyle" Benefits**—Businesses will be compelled to offer more "tailor-able" and enhanced "lifestyle" benefits to employees. We are already seeing concierge services, childcare, and eldercare offerings emerge in benefit packages. This trend will continue as a new generation of workers seeks ways to make their life easier.

6. **Incorporate Gen Y Sensibilities**—This generation of personnel is looking for fun and variety in the workplace. Let's give it to them. Certainly, we don't want to introduce utter chaos. However, promoting lightheartedness and amusement can go a long way toward improving morale and enhancing productivity (see *Clarus Marketing Group Wants You...to Have Fun*, for an example of the types of job postings that are beginning to find their way onto job boards and into want ads).

Clearly, these types of changes may seem quite radical to existing, older staff members. So, we must do our best to help them transition with us by raising their awareness of the trends taking shape in the employment market and our organizations' obvious need to leverage the opportunities that exist there.

See It in Action

Clarus Marketing Group Wants You... to Have Fun

Fueled by a recent infusion of venture capital, the ten-year-old Clarus Marketing Group of Middletown, Connecticut, is an example of a company that is positioned for growth. That said, it wants to leave its mark in the Internet services / e-commerce space by creating customized loyalty programs to help its clients build and retain a loyal customer base.

To that end, they are developing prepaid shipping services tailored to individual e-commerce websites, which will allow Clarus Marketing's clients to provide free shipping to their customers while replicating the proven success of similar programs already in use at top e-commerce portals. So, hiring for that effort and future product offerings have begun.

Interestingly, Clarus Marketing's want ad posted on the popular CareerBuilder website on January 24, 2013. not only called for:

"an experienced Senior Software Developer with deep knowledge of the .NET 4 Framework, including Visual Studio 2010, C#, ASP.NET, WCF, and ADO.NET,"

but also someone who possessed:

"experience in interoffice warfare with computer-controlled missile launchers and other 'weapons' and an obsession with sports, music, Apple products, movies, technology, or food."

Clearly, the firm is marketing its culture and promoting the fact that it wants to encourage hard work and fun.

What is more, one gets the sense that they are dead serious about interoffice warfare. A visit to their website shows three casually dressed young professionals huddled on the office floor, sitting on Yogibo beanbag chairs, sipping coffee from ceramic mugs and texting on their iPads.

The firm might as well have included another line in its want ad, *"Boring, recluses unfamiliar with Gen Y culture need not apply!"*

Nonetheless, Clarus Marketing's recruitment approach serves as an example of what businesses are beginning to do to find talent and engage would-be personnel in the strategic direction of the enterprise.

Sources:
1) http://www.clarusmarketing.com/about-clarus-marketing-group/;
2) http://www.careerbuilder.com

CHECKLIST ITEM 5: INCLUDE INCLUSION

Lest we forget, organizations are made up of all kinds of people from all kinds of backgrounds. The best enterprises are the ones that leverage the skills and experiences of everyone within the concern. The engagement techniques provided here are intended to be broadly applicable. However, specific strides can, and should, be taken to reach out to and include those people who may feel disenfranchised because of some real or perceived differences.

In my previous book, I outlined a series of steps that an executive leader can take to ensure that he or she fields a broadly diverse and inclusive workforce. Some of the ideas delineated there include:[2]

✓ re-examining job postings and descriptions (adjusting them as needed) to ensure that they truly reflect the skills and talents needed by the organization and that they don't somehow limit competent people from applying;
✓ making certain that all promotional materials visually reflect diversity and inclusion;
✓ using diversity-related success stories in company public relations campaigns;

✓ sponsoring and participating in ethnic studies programs at local colleges;

✓ place college interns and co-op students who represent diverse groups;

✓ establishing associations with government programs that train and develop diverse groups;

✓ designing and promoting employee referral processes that will serve to introduce prospective employees to the firm;

✓ ensuring that the organization provides diversity training, establishes a diversity charter, and rewards diversity efforts within the enterprise.

All of these techniques can be employed to establish a diverse organization that seeks to attract and leverage the best people available. By making diversity and inclusiveness a priority, we improve the odds of engaging more staff members in the transformation process. Take a look at ***Diversity and Inclusion Is Just Part of the Business at Marriott,*** for how one major hotelier has made diversity and inclusion a priority—a characteristic that has set the firm apart from many of its competitors.

See It in Action

Diversity and Inclusion is just Part of the Business at Marriott

Marriott International values its associates and recognizes that its global workforce is a key to its success. The firm's overarching philosophy is "Take care of our associates so they can take care of our guests." One of the ways in which it ensures that its associates are taken care of is through its diversity and inclusion programs.

Because of this focus, Marriott International has won many prestigious awards for its inclusion efforts. Here's just a sample of the more that 40 honors that it has received in the past three years:

From 2012:

✓ The National Urban League "2012 Corporate Circle Award"

✓ Named a Best Company for Hourly Workers by *Working Mother Magazine*

✓ Ranked # 3 in United Arab Emirates' Great Places to Work Survey

✓ Ranked # 1 in Supplier Diversity by *Diversity Inc.*

From 2011:

✓ Named to "World's Best Multinational Workplaces" List by Great Place to Work Institute

✓ Named Best Corporation Member of the Year by the government of China

✓ *Black Enterprise Magazine's* Top "40 Best Companies for Diversity"

✓ Recognized by the Migration Policy Institute

✓ Recognized by Capital Area Gay & Lesbian Chamber of Commerce

From 2010:

✓ Named Company of the Year by *Latina Style*

✓ *Hispanic Magazine* list of Top 25 Corporations for Supplier Diversity

✓ *Black Collegian Magazine* list of its Top 100 Employers for the Class of 2010

✓ Ranked fourth on India's "Top 25 Companies to Work for" list

There is no doubt that Marriott takes its diversity and inclusion work very seriously. Being honored like this, year after year, suggests that the firm has been more than successful in its efforts. Clearly, diversity and inclusion have become as much a part of Marriott's culture as clean sheets and fresh coffee.

Source: http://www.marriott.com/diversity/diversity-awards.mi

CHECKLIST ITEM 6: TIE ENGAGEMENT TO MEASUREMENT & REWARD PROGRAMS

Once the engagement program is in full swing, a way to promote additional commitment among staff is to tie a reward to it. People will more likely buy into the program if they are rewarded for doing so. Therefore, we must tie engagement to the measurement and reward program. This linkage becomes the way in which we incentivize desired behaviors and gain sought-after outcomes, which, in turn, promote more engagement.

Here are some suggestions on how to ensure successful integration:

✓ **Reinterpret the vision** by identifying the key themes that underpin it (for example, outside-in perspective, team-based organizational structure, "in it together" philosophy, and so forth). These are the things on which we need their engagement. So, make it easy for staff to succinctly understand what those themes are;

✓ **Provide a "cheat sheet"** by communicating the reinterpreted themes to staff at their next scheduled performance review meetings with their supervisor or manager. In this way, staff can begin to better align their thinking about their job with the direction of the enterprise;

✓ **Make it personal** by asking each staff member to develop a personal plan for how he or she will contribute to the achievement of one or more of the vision themes through his or her role and position in the organization. This activity helps personnel draw the connection between what they do and where the firm is heading, cementing the notion within their own minds of where they will "fit" in the future;

✓ **Solicit metrics** for each item identified when reviewing their personal plans with their management. What better way to gain buy-in than to have employees determine how best to measure their performance;

✓ **Celebrate achievement** of personal goals that contribute to engagement by promoting stories about it in organizational newsletters and on intranet sites. This goes a long way toward reinforcing the behaviors that are sought in the workplace.

Organizations that can connect engagement activities to measurement and rewards programs are more likely to effectively engage and motivate employees—and a motivated workforce is desperately needed to make change happen (for more on this association, see *The World at Work Engagement Study*).

See It in Action:

The World at Work Engagement Study

World at Work is a global human resources association comprised of over 30,000 members worldwide. Founded in 1955, the association is focused on training, research, and knowledge transfer on issues related to compensation, benefits, and workforce management.

In summer 2010, World at Work published an interesting study on the relationship between employee engagement and reward programs. It found that organizations that can connect engagement to total rewards practices are more likely to effectively engage and motivate employees.

Inherently, the finding makes sense. But what was more interesting in the research was the discovery that:

✓ base pay and benefits had the overall weakest relationship with the organization's ability to foster high levels of employee engagement compared to incentives, intangible rewards, and quality of leadership on engagement;

✓ although more frequent use of employee opinion surveys was associated with effectiveness in fostering high levels of employee engagement and motivation, the relationship was much stronger for organizations in which employee opinion survey results generate action and change;

✓ organizations that involve employees in the design, implementation, and assessment of total rewards programs are associated with rewards strategies that effectively engage employees.

Considering these findings, it is essential that we employ staff in the design and implementation of engagement measurement programs; ensure that the awards developed within such programs focus on intangible rewards like work-setting improvements and career enhancement elements, and that we actively incorporate program improvement suggestions that we receive from the rank and file.

By taking this approach, we will gain staff engagement, improve motivation, and breed commitment to our shared vision for the future.

Sources: The Impact of Rewards Programs on Employee Engagement by Dow Scott and Tom McMullen, World at Work, http://www.worldatwork.org/waw /adimLink?id=39032, June 2010.

TO CLOSE

Most people long for increased responsibility and continued opportunities to advance in their jobs. Indeed, many yearn to be recognized as a standout performer among their peers. We must engage our personnel in the change processes needed to eliminate the bureaucratic controls that can stifle performance and hinder a staff member's ability to be recognized for his or her accomplishments.

By making a conscientious effort to engage staff in our transformation efforts, we enable hale and hearty work environments to take seed and propagate—environments in which individual strengths are not only acknowledged but are also capitalized upon, in which every staff member has the opportunity to display his or her talents and contribute to the achievement of the strategic vision of the organization.

5

MANAGE WORK THROUGH PROJECTS—A MEANS TO STRATEGIC ALIGNMENT

Vision without execution is hallucination.

—Thomas Edison

Our next *Executive Checklist* item is about execution. Specifically, it proffers that all of the work necessary to achieving the vision for the future should be organized and managed as a portfolio of projects and programs to be accomplished over time. After all, our vision doesn't do much good if we never staff and fund the work needed to realize it.

Strictly speaking, one can think of a project portfolio as a device used to administer an organization's strategic plan. There is better alignment of strategies and implementation effort within a concern when a project portfolio approach is used as a means to direct and control strategic initiatives. Execution is made easier because project portfolio work brings with it a set of methods and disciplines that enable improved project planning and monitoring.

When portfolio management is fully embraced by an enterprise, larger efforts are more readily broken into smaller, more manageable ones. Further, project-specific issues, which may impact desired results, are discovered and addressed sooner—before they grow into larger problems that become more expensive to fix down the road.

In addition, the organization is less apt to squander precious resources on impractical and half-baked ideas when a more methodical approach is in place and functional, positioning the firm to more purposefully manage its resources and harvest expected benefits from its projects and programs.

The checklist below summarizes the essentials needed to successfully implement Project Portfolio Management (PPM):

Project Portfolio Management Checklist

✓ Know Your Starting Point.
✓ Initiate the Project Portfolio.
✓ Integrate Project Portfolio Management and Strategic Planning Processes.
✓ Reinforce through Integrated Administration.
✓ Establish Common Language.
✓ Establish Common Artifacts.
✓ Find Tools to Make It Easier.
✓ Follow the Ten Commandments.

Let us dig a little deeper into this checklist in order to reach a more complete understanding of the important concepts, implications, and underpinnings of managing work as a portfolio of projects.

CHECKLIST ITEM 1: KNOW YOUR STARTING POINT

The actions that you need to take to institutionalize PPM differ depending on where the organization is on its strategic planning and project management maturity curves. In fact, combining these two factors into one maturity model provides a quicker way to diagnose what is needed to implement portfolio management.

Here are the basic components of a simple maturity model that I have used to assist clients in developing their project portfolio implementation plans:

✓ **Stage 1**: *Foundation-Setting*—No formal strategic planning or project management methodology is in place. Therefore, it is essential that a strict program plan to implement each process and begin the work necessary to begin the practice of strategic planning and PPM is established.

✓ **Stage 2**: *Fundamentals-Building*—Some strategic planning and project management practices are being used. However, the processes are practiced in an inconsistent manner, and additional training and supporting infrastructure are needed to ensure the ongoing sophistication of both processes. Thus the program plans required for both must stress the basics and focus on building fundamental knowledge and needed organizational structure.

✓ **Stage 3**: *Practice Optimization*—An appropriate infrastructure for strategic planning and project management is in place. Detailed strategic plans exist and are maintained. Projects have been identified and are organized into a portfolio for easier administration. Processes must be fine-tuned, and additional integration points must be established to ensure full strategic alignment.

✓ **Stage 4**: *Mastery*—Very chic strategic planning and PPM processes are in place. They have been integrated and supported through automated tools. They are well managed by highly trained professionals who understand all of the idiosyncrasies inherent in the processes.

The ultimate goal is to establish strategic planning and PPM practices as core competencies within the enterprise. Knowing your starting point is essential to creating the "right" plan to make that happen. Many organizations are somewhere between Stages 1 and 2—performing some form of strategic planning and project management. However, most still lack infrastructure, and few have tightly integrated the two processes, making the deliberate planning of evolution along the maturity curve essential to enduring achievement (see **Marriott Continues up the PPM Maturity Curve**, for an example of how one firm continues to evolve its PPM competencies).

Once the starting point is determined, it is time to begin the work of instituting the PPM process.

See It in Action

Marriott Continues up the PPM Maturity Curve

The Marriott operates more than 3,700 properties worldwide and employs 129,000 people in 70 countries. To suggest that Marriott's business model is complex is an understatement. In fact, according to Marriott's Leslie Scott, vice president, Information Resources and Enterprise Project Management Office:

"At any one time, we have 250 to 300 projects underway...Our responsibility is to manage these projects and ensure they align with Marriott's overarching business strategy."[1]

In itself, 300 projects represent a substantial project portfolio. Add to it the global nature of some of those initiatives, and the management challenge can be unwieldy.

Clearly in Stage 3 of PPM maturity, the firm had formalized its project management practices, implemented a variety of project management tools, and organized its projects into a portfolio—all intended to assist individual project managers and their teams manage their way through most initiatives.

However, it lacked the capability to consolidate, summarize, and analyze project details across its portfolio of projects. More PPM sophistication was needed in order for Marriott to continue to be able to support and successfully execute the myriad of initiatives within its evolving strategic plan.

Therefore, Marriott set out to enable the implementation of a more refined PPM approach that would provide a unified view of its corporate projects, while promoting better strategic planning and resource allocation. Its approach was to replace individual project management tools with a fully integrated portfolio management solution, rich with features and functionality.

Working with Hewlett-Packard, Marriott incorporated the *HP Project and Portfolio Management Center* into its portfolio management practices and recast it into a premier, Stage 4 PPM process. The results were:

✓ better strategic alignment of projects to the strategic plan;

✓ enhanced project planning and resource allocation decisions;

✓ improved project manager productivity.

Today, if proposed projects don't sufficiently align with Marriott's overall business strategy, they are shelved. This helps keep the company dedicated to its vision and ensures that precious budget dollars are not needlessly misdirected on projects that may only serve to distract the enterprise and divert it from its strategic mission.

Source: "*Marriott Gains New Edge in Project Transparency, Planning,*" by Hewlett-Packard Development Company, L.P., http://h20195.www2.hp.com/V2/GetDocument.aspx?docname=4AA3–8543ENW&cc=us&lc=en, July, 2012

CHECKLIST ITEM 2: INITIATE THE PROJECT PORTFOLIO

As explained in Chapter 3, the strategic plan is comprised of a set of well-documented projects and programs that are intended to bridge the gap between where an organization is today and where it wants to go in the future as outlined by its vision. The PPM process comes into play once that set of initiatives is identified. For all intents and purposes, the de facto project portfolio consists of those projects and programs born through the strategic plan.

Recognizing that the strategic plan is, indeed, simply a portfolio of projects that will (once implemented) dictate how work is done within the organization is the first step toward introducing the PPM practices needed to oversee project execution, a crucial part of ensuring that the enterprise is well positioned to implement new products, services, and capabilities while modifying operations as called out in its strategic plan.

Keep in mind, the adoption of a PPM approach as a means to overseeing the execution of the strategic plan brings with it additional administrative and procedural items to be settled on. For instance, the organization must make certain that all of the initiatives in the portfolio are fully understood by the management team, and that there is a process by which to address any unintended organizational conflicts that may impact project priority-setting.

Further, provisions must be made to appropriately manage the portfolio, reliably train and nurture skills development, and properly communicate portfolio information in order to expose the firm's workforce to this new way of organizing and performing work within the enterprise and to ensure tight alignment between portfolio management and strategic planning practices (take a look at *Portfolio Management Is a Hot Topic at This Store*, for a sample of what one retailer is doing to improve its information technology [IT] project outcomes).

See It in Action

Portfolio Management Is a Hot Topic at This Store

Hot Topic, Inc., based in Los Angeles, California, offers band-related apparel and accessories, licensed merchandise, and fashion apparel and teen-based accessories through its more than 600 retail stores. Like many fast-growing concerns, the company routinely was late and over budget on its IT initiatives, which sometimes cost the retailer millions of dollars in savings and revenue.

When confronted with implementing a $3 million multiproject, integrated retail technology system, intended to tie together store operations and inventory management functions, Hot Topic had to change the way in which it was approaching project management. It could not afford for this system to be delayed or exceed budget.

The company recognized that putting the "right" resources on a given project task at the "right" time (within a specific project) would be the only way to ensure that the multiple projects that comprised the system effort coalesced properly and would be delivered as planned. The firm set out to establish a PPM environment with the capability to visualize, analyze, and optimize multiple project plans within its project portfolio.

With the help of a vendor and the implementation of some PPM tools, Hot Topic delivered the integrated retail system two weeks ahead of schedule. In addition, the retailer has reported savings of over $1 million related to improved project staffing models and quicker project completions which facilitate speedier business expansion.

Not bad, for a company that prides itself on selling Batman bikinis and Justin Bieber slim-fitting T-shirts!

Source: "Hot Topic," by ProModel Corporation http://www.promodel.com/pdf/Project%20Review%20-%20Hot%20Topic.pdf, April 11, 2012.

CHECKLIST ITEM 3: INTEGRATE PROJECT PORTFOLIO MAN-AGEMENT AND STRATEGIC PLANNING PROCESSES

As described earlier in the book, strategic planning is a continuous process that is driven and monitored by the executives in charge of the organization. The alignment of strategy and execution is safeguarded by integrating the strategic planning process, which defines direction, with the PPM process, which accelerates performance. Their alignment is a crucial element of establishing a platform for continuous transformation and strategic evolution.

It would seem obvious that the two processes should be integrated. However, they often remain separated in organizations that do perform both of them. The reasons for this vary, but commonly, the explanation for separating them stems from the different locations within the enterprise in which the processes are typically managed. Strategic planning happens at the executive layer, and PPM is usually managed from the middle layer of the organization. This has to change.

The underlying activities associated with both of these major processes should be extended in such a way as to promote solid integration. For example, the procedure for identifying and documenting a new strategic initiative should tie to a corresponding project planning activity that ratifies inclusion of it in the organization's project portfolio.

Likewise, business rules and operating procedures must be established for each process that produces the desired degree of unification between strategic planning and PPM. This implies that the executives responsible for planning are regularly meeting with the staff members responsible for portfolio management, enabling easy adjustments of the processes based on their maturation within the concern.

CHECKLIST ITEM 4: REINFORCE THROUGH INTEGRATED ADMINISTRATION

The linkage between strategic planning and PPM can be appropriately reinforced by establishing a single point for administration of both processes. Stated another way, combining the responsibilities for strategic plan administration with those of PPM will enable the desired alignment of the two major processes.

Here is an outline of the major responsibilities of an integrated strategic planning and project portfolio administration function:

✓ regularly reviewing strategic plan and project / program status (including project plans and budgets)
✓ conducting monthly executive portfolio review meetings
✓ managing the project portfolio using appropriate processes and systems
✓ updating and publishing the strategic plan
✓ communicating the strategic plan changes to the stakeholder community, as appropriate
✓ conducting biweekly project coordination meetings with project managers
✓ facilitating cross-project sharing of information and solutions among project teams
✓ identifying opportunities to consolidate project work efforts
✓ updating and improving project management policies and procedures
✓ assisting project managers in adjusting their project plans

The integrated administration function should be sized appropriately for the organization. For instance, a multinational business may need dozens of staff members working cohesively in a decentralized manner, while a smaller entity may only require a single person to play the role. Regardless of size, however, the administration function is best placed within the upper echelon of the organization in order for it to carry a suitable degree of influence and authority—important traits to possess in order for it to be most effective.

CHECKLIST ITEM 5: ESTABLISH A COMMON LANGUAGE

Another important aspect of institutionalizing PPM (and a project-centered culture, in general) is to forge a common language in order to communicate more effectively on project-related matters. This enables fuller understanding among staff and enhances performance when a recognized shorthand for communicating is established.

Certainly, most of us are familiar with basic project-related jargon, like project, project manager, project team. Therefore, we will not spend time defining those words. However, the following terms are important to distinguish and fold into the substance of the PPM vernacular:

✓ **Strategic Plan and Portfolio Administration**: As discussed in the previous checklist item, the strategic plan and portfolio administration function is responsible for maintaining both the strategic plan and an organization's project portfolio.

✓ **Executive Steering Committee**: The executive steering committee (ESC) encompasses the senior executives responsible for establishing strategic direction and defining the projects that comprise the organization's strategic plan;

✓ **Executive Steering Committee Meeting**: Usually conducted on a monthly basis, these meetings are held between the strategic plan and portfolio administrators and the ESC. The meetings provide an opportunity for the ESC to be briefed on outstanding project issues so that those issues can be addressed. The meetings also provide an opportunity for the ESC to direct changes to the strategic plan and project portfolio so that both of those devices always reflect the organization's strategic direction.

✓ **Project Sponsor**: A project sponsor is a senior executive (ideally an ESC member) who is responsible for assuring the success of a specified project. They coach project teams, resolve organizational issues, and assist project managers in managing risks so as to improve project outcomes;

✓ **Subject Matter Experts:** Subject matter experts (SMEs) supplement the skills, experience level, and capabilities of a project team. SMEs are not considered full-fledged members of the project team. Rather, SMEs are called upon, as needed, to contribute their special knowledge to a project effort. This allows their particular expertise to be leveraged across many projects while respecting the amount of time that they dedicate to any specific project or work activity.

✓ **Project Review Panel:** A project review panel is a mechanism by which project teams can gain periodic input from their peers. Panelists are fellow employees who have been charged by the ESC to review a project team's work products as those items are being produced. Panel reviews are usually held upon completion of key project deliverables. They provide an opportunity for a team to gain insight on their work from personnel who have not been directly involved with producing it. The quality of a team's final work product can be improved by gaining an "outsider's" perspective.

For more on project review panels, check out *Building a Review Panel at the JPMorgan Chase & Company*.

✓ **Project Coordination Meeting:** A project coordination meeting is hosted by the strategic plan and portfolio administration staff, and includes all project managers who are responsible for managing an active project. Typically held biweekly, these meetings are a device that helps strategic plan and portfolio administrators to better understand project status (so they can more accurately brief the ESC and update the strategic plan and project portfolio as needed), while providing an opportunity for project managers to meet and share ideas and identify potential overlap and integration points among the projects that they are responsible for managing.

✓ **Project Stand-ups**: These are used on larger, multifaceted projects that have several subteam offshoots that are running in parallel and must be tightly coordinated in order to be successful. This quick, daily meeting (sometimes called a daily huddle) is held among project team leads. It should last no more than 15 minutes and be used to share the answers to these three questions:

- What did my subteam accomplish yesterday?
- What will my subteam do today?
- What obstacles might encumber my subteam's progress?

The time should be limited to reporting project status, which is needed to improve coordination among the project teams. Project stand-ups should not be used to resolve problems. More extensive project meetings can be scheduled to address problem resolution.

These terms represent the key rudiments of what it takes to manage work as a portfolio of projects. Perfecting the definition of and establishing a standard set of project artifacts is just as important to the institutionalization of PPM.

See It in Action

Building a Review Panel at the JPMorgan Chase & Company

A few years ago, I helped the Corporate Client Banking division of JPMorgan Chase with some strategic planning and, together with a small team of their planners, we established a project review panel in order to enage staff members more widely in the project portfolio work that resulted.

Here are the guidelines that were established for the project review panel process:

- ✓ A review panel is comprised of no fewer than six and no more than eight staff members.
- ✓ The panel encompasses staff from across the company and all reporting levels.
- ✓ Only a few hours per month (for example, typically four to eight hours / month) will be required of a panelist.
- ✓ Once fully established, panelists will be asked to participate over the course of a six-month rotation.

✓ The replacement of those who are asked to be on the inaugural review panel may be staggered so as to provide ongoing continuity on the panel as its membership evolves over time.

✓ Panel reviews will be scheduled into each project's task list.

✓ Typically, a panel review will be conducted by a project team upon completion of each major milestone.

✓ Panelists are expected to raise important questions / issues and provide an "outsider's point of view" to each project team.

✓ Panelists are expected to communicate and discuss what they are learning about the projects with their peers so as to promote better communication within the company.

✓ The review panel has no approval or sign-off responsibilities. Its sole purpose is to provide additional input to project teams.

While this is a modest set of operating principles for a 200-year-old financial powerhouse with assets of over $2.3 trillion, they served to get the project portfolio process off the ground.

CHECKLIST ITEM 6: ESTABLISH COMMON ARTIFACTS

According to the *American Heritage Dictionary*, an artifact is "*an object produced or shaped by human craft, especially a tool, weapon, or ornament of archaeological or historical interest.*"[2] Projects produce artifacts in the form of work products that organizations use to enable the achievement of their strategic vision. It is essential that we insist on establishing a common set of project artifacts to be crafted in **every** project so as to provide the uniformity of practice and standardization needed to capably manage a large portfolio of projects. Otherwise, inconsistencies and chaos can result within the project portfolio.

Here is a preliminary set of project artifacts that I routinely recommend to my clients when we are developing a PPM program:

✓ **Project Brief**: Used for planning purposes, a project brief summarizes the objectives of a project that is under consideration by the Executive Steering Committee. The brief describes what will be delivered and how the initiative will be carried out. Once approved for inclusion in the strategic plan, the project is staffed, funded, and added to the project portfolio. The project brief is used by the strategic plan and portfolio administrators and the assigned project manager to develop the project plan.

✓ **Project Plan:** A project plan is a set of tasks to be performed within specified time frames (that is, target or due dates) in order to produce the desired work products. Typically, these tasks are organized into phases that, when completed, produce a specified project deliverable. The specification of the tasks, dates, and deliverables are an essential element of managing the project portfolio and coordinating project interdependencies that exist within it.

✓ **Project Status Report:** A project status report contains information about the current state of a project. Produced on a weekly basis by each project manager, it is collected and tracked by the strategic plan and portfolio administration function. The report helps the administration function manage the project portfolio. It provides an audit trail that documents projects' progress from their inception to completion.

✓ **Project Delay Report:** The project delay report is an exception report that is created only when a project team finds that it is running behind schedule on its project plan. The report describes the delay, estimates the impact on completion dates, and documents the steps that will be taken to get the project back on track. Project delay reports contribute to project documentation and assist in portfolio management activities.

✓ **Portfolio Health Bulletin:** The portfolio health bulletin is produced monthly by the strategic plan and portfolio administration function. Intended to provide a dashboard for use by the executive team, it presents the overall status of the organization's project portfolio. Further, when automated tools are available, the bulletin is delivered in electronic form. Regardless of the delivery vehicle, these reports use color-coded Gantt charting and provide links to project detail drill-down capabilities so as to ensure complete understanding of the portfolio.

✓ **Project Interdependency Journal**: The project interdependency journal captures project dependencies that exist among the projects in a concern's project portfolio. Fashioned on-demand by the strategic plan and portfolio administration function, the journal cross-references projects and helps to determine shifting priorities as the portfolio evolves. Together with the portfolio health bulletin, the journal is an important portfolio management instrument.

As you can imagine, these types of project artifacts can accumulate fairly quickly in a modest-sized project portfolio. The challenge of producing and tracking these essential documents becomes more unruly as portfolios grow and advance over time. Therefore, finding and implementing tools that make project management and portfolio administration easier is essential to long-term success (see *AmSurg Brings Order to Its Project Portfolio*, for a real-world example of some of the automated portfolio administration competencies in action).

See It in Action

AmSurg Brings Order to its Project Portfolio

"The ability to perform procedures at the same high level of care with the same specialized attention as hospitals, but at a lower cost" is AmSurg's value proposition.

The company is a nationally recognized leader in the development, management and operation of outpatient surgery centers. They do business at more than 220 outpatient surgery centers in 35 states, offering patients a comfortable environment in which they can receive convenient, personal, and high-quality treatment at a low cost. At any time, the firm has multiple projects in motion within virtually every department, many intended for rollout to all of AmSurg surgery centers throughout the country. AmSurg needed a way to track and manage the projects and programs they were undertaking.

However, the company lacked organizational project management knowledge and had little governance in place. Yet executive demand for project status and for tracking information continued to increase due to the pace and costs associated with widespread project execution. AmSurg needed an automated PPM solution.

After evaluating various product offerings, the company selected BrightWork, a computerized package that leverages Microsoft's Share-Point platform (a technology that AmSurg already had in place and understood). Within no time, AmSurg had customized the project portfolio product to fit the way they managed projects.

Today, the firm uses the system to store all project-related work, including project plans, budgets, issues documents, and status reports. Senior management uses the built-in dashboard reporting feature to track specific efforts, while a portfolio view provides a snapshot of all active projects and allows managers to check statuses without having to navigate through the SharePoint environment to find them.

Like the firm's value proposition, AmSurg's use of PPM technology allows it to manage its project portfolio at a high level, but at a lower cost. Isn't that what we all want to achieve in our project management work?

Source: "Project and Portfolio Management using SharePoint," by Bright-Work, http://www.brightwork.com/case_studies/index.htm, April 12, 2012

CHECKLIST ITEM 7: FIND TOOLS TO MAKE IT EASIER

There are whole host of product offerings available within the PPM space (see *PPM's Varied Choices*, for a small sample of vendor offerings). PPM tools should be considered as separate and distinct from those that are aimed at supporting strictly project management (which are equally plentiful in the marketplace). After all, the tools needed to manage work as a portfolio of projects is different from the automated support required to track and manage an individual project endeavor.

That said, here is a list of the general categories of essential features and functions that are of import to PPM:

✓ **Portfolio Administration:** Important capabilities to seek include access rights and security management, project prioritization and selection support, project dependency itemization, trend analysis, multi-year scenario planning support, and portfolio risk analysis

✓ **Portfolio Information Management:** Important capabilities to seek include multiproject and user support, project artifact storage and retrieval, key project plan item search, data archiving, and data import/export functionality

✓ **Project Evaluation:** Important capabilities to seek include financial analysis (for example, Net Present Value, Internal Rate of Return, and so forth), capture and monitoring of nonfinancial benefits, postmortem reporting. and lessons learned tracking

✓ **Resource Management:** Important capabilities to seek include individual resource skillset tracking (by physical location), resource request management and selection, resource assignment tracking, resource demand monitoring, and analysis and time-tracking

✓ **Reporting Functions:** Important capabilities to seek include a solid package of predefined reports, multidimensional ad-hoc reporting functionality, user-defined dashboard views, data-drill down facility, and scheduled report creation and delivery features

✓ **Communication and Collaboration Support:** Important capabilities to seek include integrated user assistance and help capabilities, bulk- and cross-portfolio communication functionality (that is, to all project managers and stakeholders), and real-time and rules-based communication features

See It in Action

PPM's Varied Choices

There are literally hundreds of automated PPM tools available in the marketplace. Offerings come from companies big and small. For illustrative purposes, here is a very small list of PPM product offerings organized by vendor size.

Offerings from Larger Vendors:

✓ *CA Clarity PPM* is available from **CA Technologies**. It offers an integrated product suite that organizes PPM information and processes into a single system of record.

✓ *HP Project and Portfolio Management* is available from **Hewlett-Packard**. It offers an integrated set of tools for presenting varied portfolio views across both traditional and agile projects.

✓ *Project Server 2013* is available from **Microsoft**. It offers an on-premises solution for PPM that drives cross-project collaboration through an integrated SharePoint solution.

✓ *Rational Focal Point* is available from **IBM**. It offers visualization, prioritization, road mapping, and planning capabilities through an integrated set of tools.

✓ *SAP Portfolio and Project Management* is available from **SAP**. It offers a product suite that links project data, workflows, and business processes intended to better manage the project portfolio.

Offerings from Smaller Vendors:

✓ *OneDesk* is available from **OneDesk, Inc.** It offers a comprehensive SaaS-based project management application that facilitates PPM.

✓ *Portfolio Simulator* is available from **ProModel Corporation**. It offers a product that is intended to bridge the communication gap between top-down and bottom-up planning so as to better align planning with PPM.

✓ *Project Insight* is available from **Metafuse, Inc.** It offers an integrated, web-based project portfolio, project management, resource management, and collaboration suite.

✓ *Project.net* is available from **Integrated Computer Solutions, Inc.** It offers an open-source tool to capture, display, report on, and resolve complex project interrelationships with a project portfolio.

✓ *Projectplace* is available from **Projectplace International**. It offers cloud-based PPM and project team collaboration capabilities through its product offering.

Keep in mind, this is just a small fraction of the toolsets available. Time should be taken and careful thought given when sorting through so many varied options.

When evaluating commercially available tools, keep in mind that vendor offerings differ significantly in the methods by which, and how well, they deliver the previously mentioned automated capabilities. Proper screening can be accomplished through product demonstrations, reference checking, and pilot programming. Be sure to weave these elements into your tool-selection process

For more on product evaluation criteria, please see *"Choosing the Right PPM Tools for You."*

See It in Action

Choosing the Right PPM Tools for You

It can be quite a challenge to weed through all of the current PPM product offerings. Certainly, the purchase price and features and functions available within the toolsets are of paramount importance. However, it may be worth adding these frequently overlooked selection criteria to your PPM product evaluation screen:

✓ total cost of operation
✓ ease of use
✓ learning curve
✓ product platform (that is, operating system, hardware requirements, and so forth)
✓ product delivery model (for example, single-user desk-top, multi-user server-based, web-based, hosted, or Software-as-a-Service)
✓ product's stated future direction

✓ vendor's service delivery proficiencies
✓ vendor's reputation and financial status

With so many options available, it is important to develop a standard way to appraise vendor product suites. By integrating these selection criteria with those aimed at evaluating key features and functions, you will improve your chances of making the "right" long-term choice for your organization.

CHECKLIST ITEM 8: FOLLOW THE TEN COMMANDMENTS

A few years ago, I wrote a piece for *Computerworld*[3] that outlined the ten commandments of project management. I would be remiss if I did not share the commandments here. Thankfully, they still apply and are an appropriate complement to our discussion of PPM. The ten commandments of project management are summarized below:

1. **Thou Shalt the Narrow Project Scope**

   To keep projects tight and focused, carve larger efforts into smaller projects that have achievable deliverables and can meet deadlines.

2. **Thou Shalt Not Suffer a Fat Team**

   There is no optimum team size, though smaller is better. If you can double up on the roles a person plays on the team, the better.

3. **Thou Shalt Require Full-Time Business Participation**

   By committing full-time resources to every project, business leaders confirm that project work is important.

4. **Thou Shalt Establish Project Review Panels**

   As discussed earlier in the chapter, a project review panel is a project team's governing body, addressing issues of business policy and strategic direction while assisting in the removal and avoidance of project roadblocks and pitfalls.

5. **Thou Shalt Not Provoke Burnout**

   One common contributor to burnout is serial project assignments. Be sensitive to this and "share the wealth" by using a wide variety of personnel on projects over time.

6. **Thou Shalt Seek Outside Assistance as Needed**

   It's essential to bring the right consulting support to a project at the right time. Outside project management and planning professionals can often provide valuable new ideas, perspective, and energy.

7. **Thou Shalt Empower Project Teams**

   Project teams should be empowered to do whatever it takes to get a superior job completed on time and within budget.

8. **Thou Shalt Use Project Management Tools**

   Look for tools that offer project tracking, task management, workflow administration, and resource-analysis support on a web or an intranet-based platform.

9. **Thou Shalt Recognize and Reward Success**

   All project participants should be recognized in some positive way for their toil and personal sacrifice. The rewards need not be extravagant, but they must be sincere. See *A Project Showcase at DRS*, for a modest example of what can be done.

10. **Thou Shalt Not Tolerate Quick-and-Dirty Work Efforts**

    Quick and dirty means short on planning and tight on deadlines. This type of project approach only leads to error, waste, rework, and frustration. Avoid it at all costs.

By overlaying these project management guidelines on the PPM structure discussed throughout this chapter, we as executives can position our organizations for great success in the project-based culture that is emerging in today's business world.

See It in Action

A Project Showcase at DRS

Last year, we put together a strategic planning program at Connecticut's Department of Revenue Services (DRS). The pinnacle of the program was the creation of a project portfolio comprised of the many and varied initiatives that would be needed to renovate the Agency's tax collections operation. The portfolio was organized across three implementation plateaus of a year each. At the completion of the first year, we launched an effort aimed at celebrating the achievements of the completed projects that year.

The eight project managers who successfully delivered their projects were asked to prepare a brief, five-minute presentation of one slide each that highlighted what their project delivered and how it contributed to the agency's strategic vision. The project manager's material was book-ended by opening remarks from the DRS commissioner and closing comments by the deputy commissioner, demonstrating executive commitment to the project portfolio and the transformation program in general.

The one-hour Project Showcase events were held over a number of days so that every staff member could attend scheduled briefings without any disruption to the work of the Agency. Employee response to the event was outstanding. It worked to commemorate project success, while recognizing the contributions of the project managers and their teams.

Upon completion of the Project Showcase, a pizza party was held and each project manager was presented with a plaque signed by the commissioner—a small accolade in comparison to the recognition that the project managers received from their peers for a job well done—reinforcing the notion that rewards need not be extravagant as long as they are sincere.

TO CLOSE

It just makes sense to arrange of all of the work necessary to realize an organization's strategic vision into a project portfolio. A project portfolio provides a context for simplifying what is complex. It has the capacity to break larger endeavors into smaller ones that are more easily managed. It provides a framework that enables executive engagement in project execution and delivers a platform for informed decision-making, ensuring proper resource allocation and improved management and monitoring of the internal investments needed to achieve long-term business success.

When fortified by automated tools and a skilled and committed administration function, PPM is the linchpin that integrates strategic planning with project implementation—vitally securing vision to action.

Given today's competitive realities, can an organization really afford not manage its work through a portfolio of projects?

6

RENOVATE THE BUSINESS—A WAY TO BECOME "OF CHOICE"

He that will not apply new remedies must expect new evils; for time is the greatest innovator.

—Francis Bacon

Whether stated deliberately, or otherwise, every executive wants his or her organization to be "of Choice," which translates into becoming the Organization of Choice, Employer of Choice and Investment of Choice within his or her enterprise's niche, market and industry. To be "Of Choice" underpins virtually every strategic initiative that a management team imagines, staffs, funds, and executes.

Don't buy it? Consider the initiatives defined within your enterprise's current strategic plan. Are they not all aimed at differentiating your organization? Are they not about attracting more customers, enticing the best employees, gaining more investment in your enterprise? Strategy is all about being "of Choice." The challenge is how to best get there and remain preferred among all other options that exist in the marketplace.

Business renovation, the act of continuously improving on what you do as an enterprise, is a fundamental factor in becoming "of Choice." Like a world-class athlete working on fundamentals, organizations must be constantly refining and improving. It is the focus on getting better that enables our enterprises to extend current business practices and introduce new ones that are vital to strategic achievement.

The items on the checklist offered below should be considered when establishing, or enhancing, an enterprise-wide transformation program. These are good steps to follow in order to be most effective in renovating the business:

Business Renovation Checklist
✓ Renovate to differentiate.
✓ Fold it into the strategy.
✓ Choose an approach.
✓ Tackle the whole process.
✓ Eliminate the silos.
✓ Limit location dependencies.
✓ Automate whatever, whenever you can.
✓ Make it last.

Let us examine each of these checklist items, so we can better understand why business renovation is a provision for being "of Choice."

CHECKLIST ITEM 1: RENOVATE TO DIFFERENTIATE

Improvement for the sake of doing things differently is not why we as executives must establish ongoing business renovation programs within our organizations. Rather, we should renovate in order to strategically differentiate our enterprises from the competition. This distinction is an important one to make because it serves to inform the decisions about which types of changes and improvements we should pursue.

To be the organization of choice, for example, suggests that we offer the right products, at the right price, through the right distribution channels while providing the right customer experience. It does not automatically imply that we offer the lowest price or the best product in order to be "of choice." Quite the opposite, in fact. It proposes that we possess the optimum combination of elements to make our enterprise stand out within the markets in which we compete.

That's why understanding the reason for business renovation is so important. For business renovation efforts aimed at simply becoming the least expensive provider or forming the most sophisticated product portfolio may be ill-advised. A more appropriate approach may be to aim business transformation efforts at initiatives that yield the right combination of product, price, and service.

The same can be said for differentiation initiatives derived through employer and investment of choice objectives as well. It follows that a subset of the renovation program attends to establishing the right work setting, with the right culture, and the right compensation models to attract the best employees and lead the organization in a way that delivers sector-leading financial performance to its stakeholders.

By making strategic differentiation the goal of all business renovation activities, organizations will begin to push for the right kinds of changes in the way work is performed and in the way the enterprise is run. In fact, when a business transformation program is designed with "of Choice" goals in mind, improvements in virtually all areas of an organization will result.

Sometimes the search for superiority may lead to radical changes in an organization's core business. Check out *Radical Transformers* for a sampling of companies that have continually transformed both their businesses and operations through directed renovation efforts in order to remain at the top of their respective industries.

See It in Action

Radical Transformers

Here is a sample of leading organizations that have radically transformed in order to remain competitive and, in so doing, have had to continuously renovate, and in some cases overhaul, their business operations:

- ✓ **3M:** Rose to prominence in sandpaper manufacturing, but is now known for its adhesives and Post-it notes.
- ✓ **Apple** built its brand on personal computers, and now sells music and mobile phones.

✓ **Corning** mass-produced glassware, but grew its business into one that provides TV screens and cell phone covers.

✓ **DuPont** built a business making black gun powder, and now sells liners for bulletproof vests.

✓ **Fortune Brands** began with tobacco products, and now churns out golf clubs and home furnishings.

✓ **GE** started with the light bulb, and now builds jet engines and CT scanning machines.

✓ **IBM** went from selling large-scale computing machinery to providing software and consulting services.

✓ **Monsanto** once manufactured saccharine, now produces genetically engineered seeds.

✓ **Nokia** transformed from a paper, rubber, and cable works conglomerate to one that produces cell phones and computer games for mobile devices.

✓ **Xerox** made a name for itself creating photographic paper, and now fabricates printers and copy machines.

All of these companies have made dynamic changes over the years. All were renovated through a desire for strategic differentiation. Strategic differentiation must be the driver for all ongoing business transformation programs. Process improvement initiatives aimed at providing incremental change will never harvest the type of game-changing renovation needed by organizations in order to flourish and grow.

Source: "10 Companies that Radically Transformed Their Businesses," Josh Sanburn, Time: Business and Money, http://business.time.com/2011/06/16/10-companies-that-radically-transformed-their-businesses, June 16, 2011.

CHECKLIST ITEM 2: FOLD IT INTO THE STRATEGY

Just like other initiatives intended to differentiate, the business renovation program should be incorporated into the strategic plan of the enterprise. An organization should strive to do its renovation work in a standard way, using a shared set of tools and practices. The best, long-term results are achieved through business renovation programs in which common language and behaviors related to the work are established within the concern.

We as executives can hedge our bets on business transformation commonality and standardization by making a business renovation program a key strategic plan initiative. By definition, transformation is an ongoing activity that is manifested via a set of projects. Thus, it lends itself very well to be managed as a strategic program.

Once the business renovation fundamentals are in place, all business improvement projects can be added to the transformation program plan, as well. However, the first order of business is to design and deliver a program plan that identifies the steps needed to operationalize business renovation activities for continuous execution within the enterprise.

Projects intended to standardize related practices, tools, and training will be included in the business renovation program plan. After that is completed, all current and future business transformation and workflow redesign initiatives will be added to the resulting program plan. Refer to *Project Brief: The Business Renovation Program*, to see how a recent client documented the essence of its renovation program for inclusion in its strategic plan.

See It in Action

Project Brief: The Business Renovation Program

Here is a project brief developed for one of my clients during a recent strategic-planning engagement. A project brief is used to document a strategic initiative that will be included in a firm's strategic plan. The brief provides a high-level overview of the program and captures executive management's expectations of the effort:

Name: *Business Renovation Program*

Strategic Intent: The program is intended to institutionalize business transformation practices within the company and help to establish a new way of thinking about how work is done here, one that questions the status quo, while stressing continuous improvement. Intended to be an ongoing initiative, the program will commence with a focus on constructing the necessary infrastructure for business transformation work to flourish and will culminate over time with the creation of a new organizational unit that will drive the program on a formal basis going forward.

Considerations:

✓ A standard method for performing *Business Transformation* must be introduced and implemented in order to position the company for perpetual change.

✓ Staff must be trained in the firm's preferred business transformation methodology.

✓ We must evaluate the current level of customer service and satisfaction. Complementary projects must be established within the program, which identifies best-practice techniques used within the company, and those used in the industry. These projects must incorporate measurement and feedback systems that continually monitor customer service levels.

✓ As a part of every subsequent business process renovation effort, service level agreements between "internal downstream customers" must be established with a focus on the common objective of delivering superior service to our clientele.

✓ Internal operating efficiency must also be regarded as an important means to enhance the bottom line. Nonessential activities that drain vital energy and internal capacity must be eliminated. Initiatives that reduce costs, improve the workflow, and leverage technology must be introduced.

✓ Finally, early successes will be broadly recognized and celebrated within the organization in order to encourage the cultural transformation intended by executing this program.

Criticality: High

Timing: We intend to staff and fund this program within 60 days of strategic plan rollout.

At this time, the program is off and running. The client has embraced the concept of continuous renovation, and most of its early strategic initiatives have included business process redesign elements in their respective project plans, ensuring that opportunities for improvement are woven into all that they do. Folding a business renovation program into the organizational strategy, as illustrated here, is an important part of long-term cultural change, and it should be done as a matter of course when developing an enterprise's strategic plan.

CHECKLIST ITEM 3: CHOOSE AN APPROACH

Clients and prospects alike often get engaged in lengthy debates over which process improvement methodology to select for implementation. These deliberations often turn into arguments because passions flare and egos become bruised over the merits of a given Total Quality Management (TQM), Lean or Six Sigma approach.

After being part of many of these discussions, I have come to realize a dirty, little secret—it does not matter which one you choose! At the end of the day, it is more important to pick an approach and work to institutionalize it than it is to spend cycles attempting to discern the absolutely best possible improvement methodology ever invented.

That is not to say that they are all the same. There are, indeed, differences that may lend themselves to an easier implementation within a given concern. However, an organization really can't make a mistake by selecting any of them as its standard approach as long as it commits to doing the more essential work of homogenizing it for use within the enterprise. If your organization tends to get stuck on making the perfect choice, see *A Simple Selection Screen*, for some additional perspective on each of the major approaches.

It should be noted that, there are literally hundreds of vendors that specialize in delivering services in each of these methods. Many, in fact, have introduced their own twists and interpretations in order to differentiate their offerings. The selection of the "right" vendor can make or break your organization's methodology implementation.

My advice is to choose the vendor wisely. You may be better off with a management consultant, with no ties to a specific vendor or approach, to act as your general contractor. The consultant will work on your behalf to limit the risks to the overall business renovation program, by managing the methodology vendor and dealing with the clean-up work if a selected vendor proves ineffective.

See It in Action

A Simple Selection Screen

In the interest of helping my clients through the process improvement methodology selection process, I have devised the following as a "screen" of the three most popular approaches. Feel free to use it, if you find that your executive team is getting hung up over semantics.

✓ **TQM:** Total Quality Management is the granddaddy of improvement methodologies. Based on the work of early quality pioneers, including W. Edwards Deming, Joseph M. Juran, and Kaoru Ishikawa, TQM adopts a long-term, organization-wide approach to process improvement. It may be most preferred by enterprises that appreciate precision over haste and ones that relate better to *"slow and steady wins the race"* than *"ready, shoot, aim."*

✓ **Lean:** Derived from work done at Toyota in the 1990s, this approach focuses on preserving value-added activities within a process and eradicating those work steps that a customer would not be willing to pay for. It lends itself to organizations that prefer "quick hits" over sweeping change. It can deliver incremental improvements within short time frames.

✓ **Six Sigma:** Popularized by General Electric commitment to it over a decade ago, the approach uses statistical analysis to identify and eliminate the causes of defects within a given business process. An organization that identifies with the more traditional, command-and-control management structure (made popular in the military) may appreciate this technique's rigidity and use of rank designations—including green belt, orange belt and black belt—that are earned and awarded through training and experience with the methodology.

Regardless of which one is chosen, all will work masterfully as long as they are suitably implemented. So, take the time to properly institute the selected methodology within your organization.

CHECKLIST ITEM 4: TACKLE THE WHOLE PROCESS

Regardless of the methodology selected, they all possess a diagramming technique that is used to represent the workflow. The resulting drawing shows where all of the handoffs occur within a process. Eliminating handoffs improves efficiencies. Therefore, a process diagram provides a map for the "search and destroy mission" that underpins most process improvement approaches.

However, today's competitive landscape requires a bit more analysis than is needed to simply reduce the handoffs that exist within a process. An establishment's future success in renovating its business rests not on incremental improvement, but on the ability to redesign business processes that know no organizational boundaries, and on preparing workers to get the "whole job" done, regardless of organizational structure or reporting lines. Rethinking the whole process is the only means to get the edge needed to become and remain "of Choice."

I wrote about the "whole job" concept in a previous book. Let me share some of the implications that were outlined there, because they apply to our discussion as well:[1]

✓ Processes will need to be reviewed and redefined, independent of current organizational boundaries. Emphasis will need to be placed on performing the "whole job" instead of only specific pieces. Artificial boundaries that promote a "silo" mentality (see next section for more complete definition) need to be eliminated.

✓ Jobs will be redefined. All attendant responsibilities and commitments related to performing the "whole job" will need to be folded into job specifications.

✓ Managers will need education on how to manage the process to optimize results rather than managing the activities of people performing the work. The game is won by gaining the expected results, not by micromanaging the work of each employee.

✓ Projects aimed at re-engineering selected business processes will be necessary to ensure that "best practices" and other quality standards are designed into new processes.

✓ Business redesign strategies will need to be adopted to continue the improvement effort on an ongoing basis.

✓ Educating employees about new organization designs, process definition, and job responsibilities is essential in gaining buy-in and reducing feelings of friction or alienation that often come with change.

It is imperative that we tackle the whole process, and nothing but the whole process, when endeavoring to transform our organizations. Incremental improvements will never add up to the sweeping changes required to enable the level of breakthrough thinking and strategy formulation required to stay competitive for years to come.

CHECKLIST ITEM 5: ELIMINATE THE SILOS

Once the method for driving business renovation is in place, an organization can set about the work of actually analyzing what it does and how it does it, so as to identify ways to improve its major operations.

When working on large-scale business transformation initiatives, it is important to identify the "organizational silos" that exist within the entity as early as possible. They tend to be sources for immediate improvement and impact.

An organizational silo is a work unit or department that places priority on the achievement of its own parochial interests over the larger objectives of the enterprise. It has adopted this behavior as a protection mechanism intended to preserve what it does from interference from anything that could disturb how it operates.

To illustrate, consider a company that has conflict between its sales department (responsible for selling products to customers) and its operations department (responsible for making the products that customers purchase). Driven to meet sales goals, the sales department routinely make promises to customers that the operations department cannot keep, placing undue pressure on another organizational unit to make its goals. This type of silo behavior contributes to organizational dysfunction and leads to deep-rooted customer dissatisfaction—a surefire way to **NOT** be "of Choice."

What's more, because silos tend to horde information and control communication flow, they tend to be wildly inefficient and, often, disruptive to organizational performance. Thus, their redesign or elimination can be truly transformative for an enterprise seeking long-term improvements in the ways and means of execution.

Identifying and eliminating organizational silos is the first thing that I recommend when working with clients on business renovation projects. Silos can be reconsidered by introducing a team-based approach that commingles various disciplines into teams so as to eliminate the protectionist behaviors of the silo mentality that is so harmful to business performance. See *Redefining State Government*, for a recent example.

See It in Action

Redefining Connecticut State Government

As mentioned in Chapter 3, Connecticut's tax department (known as the Department of Revenue Services [DRS]) is headed up by a forward-thinking leadership team. Rosemary Cleary is one the Agency's newly minted senior executives. In fall 2012, Cleary was put in charge of the Agency's Operations Bureau, which is responsible for processing tax returns and administering the appropriate billing and refunds associated with each return.

As you can imagine, processing millions of returns annually that cover the state's more than 50 tax types can be arduous. Sanctioned by her commissioner, she decided to sponsor a business renovation initiative aimed at improving the way returns were processed within her bureau. The effort yielded recommendations for a complete overhaul of the Operations organization.

As a result of years of inattention, the Operations Bureau was peppered with organizational silos that made it less than efficient and subject to backlogs and waste. Therefore, our project team, comprised of players from within the bureau and representatives from other parts of the Agency, decided that the best way to gain lasting improvement would be to break down the silos and reorganize the bureau's 12 business units into 8 cross-functional teams.

Representing radical thinking by any stretch of the imagination, the recommendation was met with initial skepticism. Questions regarding its practicality, likelihood of success, and impact on morale were top of mind. The fact that the Bureau was comprised of unionized workers did not make the discussions any easier. However, after some deliberation, it was decided that the team-based structure was the right answer for the Agency.

The changes were put into place following the April 2013 tax season. There were a few bumps in the road, and adjustments were made to accommodate them. However, the changes as a whole have been viewed as a great success, and Connecticut's tax department is readying for another successful tax season with its team-based Operations Bureau heading the way.

CHECKLIST ITEM 6: LIMIT LOCATION DEPENDENCIES

Like organizational silos, location dependencies can stifle performance and growth. A location dependency is a business condition that requires an organization to run some part of its operations in a specific geographical location, which limits its ability to change and adapt. For example, a company that has a 500,000-square-foot physical plant packed with heavy-duty two-ton machinery cannot quickly and easily pick up stakes and move the factory to another locale. Its manufacturing business is currently location dependent.

Sniffing out location dependencies and determining ways to limit the degree to which an organization is reliant on a specific geographical location leads to the types of broad changes needed to become a more agile organization, one that can adjust on a dime to meet market needs and respond swiftly and effectively to customer demands and desires.

After some business renovation work, the company referenced in the example above, for instance, may determine that the best way for it to remain "of Choice" in the marketplace is to be location independent and shift from its centralized in-house manufacturing model to a decentralized, outsourced model, leveraging a network of outside manufacturers to deliver their products to their customers on-demand (see *H&M's Fast Fashion Business Model*, for a concrete illustration of the concept).

Of course, there are other considerations, beyond physical plant, to contemplate when working to establish more location independence. Decisions about workflow design, staff location and training, alterations in supervisory responsibility, and the creative use of technology and automation all come into play during the analysis of the enterprise. The conclusions drawn and recommendations developed will impact and inform an organization's future composition and strategic direction well into the future.

See It in Action

H&M's Fast Fashion Business Model

H&M is a Sweden-based clothing retailer. With over 2,600 stores operating in 43 countries, this multinational organization employs over 60,000 people, making it the second-largest global clothing retailer in the world. Because it offers products in all major market segments, including men's, women's, and children's fashion, the company fights for market share with rivals big and small.

Known for its "fast fashion" business model, a term used by clothing retailers to indicate a business strategy that is based on the philosophy of moving the latest fashion designs from catwalk to store in the fastest time and at the best price point possible, the firm realized a few years ago that rivals like Zara and Benetton were beginning to beat them to the punch.

H&M decided to explore ways to renovate its business. It started in manufacturing and determined that it no longer needed to do that function in-house. In fact, it realized that owning its own production operations limited its ability to move quickly on new designs, and it tied them to specific locations that would regularly need to be moved in order to accommodate growth and take advantage of lower cost labor pools.

Thus, H&M adopted a new approach that leverages a network of nearly 800 factories located in Europe and Asia to whom H&M has outsourced the manufacturing work. The H&M management team orchestrates production from the company's Stockholm headquarters. In this way, H&M maintains control of activities like merchandise planning and product design and specification—the same ones that set it apart from its competitors—and leaves the less creative work of manufacturing to its outsourcing partners.

This change in approach allows H&M to be quicker to market and less location dependent, while dramatically lowering overhead expenses—an outcome that every enterprise seeks to achieve. It is another stellar example of business renovation at its best.

CHECKLIST ITEM 7: AUTOMATE WHATEVER, WHENEVER YOU CAN

It is amazing to consider the degree to which organizations are automating their core business functions. A glimpse at *Athlete's Performance, Inc. Automates Its Brain Trust* helps make the point. The firm has actually captured the knowledge of its expert trainers and therapists within an automated system, making it broadly available for all staff to use and leverage.

However, because business renovation initiatives exhaustively examine the way work is performed, it is not uncommon for such transformation programs to generate long lists of automation opportunities for the enterprise. This inevitably raises a question: *"Where do we begin?"*

Clearly, no organization can automate everything all at once. A common approach is to identify the most impactful opportunities and tackle them first. There is no denying the merit in this kind of thinking. However, it is important to recognize that that approach comes with risks. After all, some of the most important projects often come with hefty price tags and longer time frames—both put undue stress on an organization that can lead to huge project busts.

Many of my clients have adopted a different approach to automation opportunity prioritization. Many executive teams have chosen to embrace a concept that calls for automating whatever, whenever they can. That is not to say that these concerns don't have long-term computing technology strategies. They do have automation plans that integrate nicely with their strategies (more on this in the next chapter).

However, their philosophy calls for breaking down larger computing initiatives into smaller ones—where risks can be better anticipated and managed—and fitting those efforts into a collection of "quick-hit" systems projects that offer only modest improvements to the enterprise, but that can be done quickly and easily.

These organizations have opted for a "slow and steady" approach over the "big bang theory." As a result, it has been my experience that more automation is fielded by those enterprises over the long run than by the organizations that choose to tackle only a few really big computing projects at a time.

See It in Action

Athlete's Performance, Inc. Automates Its Brain Trust

Founded in 1999, Athletes' Performance, Inc. came into prominence in sports circles by providing integrated training, nutrition, mental conditioning, and physical therapy programs to professional and elite athletes from around the globe from its four locations in the United States. Their high-profile clients visit Athletes' Performance to take advantage of the high-quality services delivered by the company's team of experts.

Recently, the company decided to expand its integrated fitness offerings for inclusion in corporate wellness programs. Implicit in the approach was the challenge of how to best leverage its wealth of knowledge across Athletes' Performance's various specialties so as to create personalized programs for members of client companies.

It moved to employ an automated approach that would centralize the knowledge currently stored in the minds of its in-house staff of behavioral science, fitness, and physical therapy experts. Through the process of knowledge engineering, the firm was able to create an automated system that utilizes the rules captured through its knowledge engineering efforts to customize individual fitness and nutritional programs for corporate wellness clients.

The results have been phenomenal. The automation effort has led to a customer retention rate of 92 percent, and it has enabled efficiencies that allow a single performance specialist to work with 16 clients at a time. By centralizing much of the knowledge that Athletes' Performance's experts provide when coaching its elite clientele, it has effectively found a way to leverage decades of experience for use by a larger audience.

Who would have guessed that what are widely considered "high touch" processes, like athletic coaching and behavioral counseling, could be automated to enable competitive gain? This demonstrates that adopting an "automate whatever, whenever you can" philosophy can pay dividends when approached through a business renovation lens.

Source: IBM Software Case Studies: Athletes' Performance—Gets People Fit with Scalable Technology, **ibm.com**/brms, June 2, 2011.

CHECKLIST ITEM 8: MAKE IT LAST

As you might imagine, there is strong resistance to most business renovation efforts because they represent change. We all know that no one likes to change. Most people resist it for as long as they can. Thus, long-range, ongoing transformation programs can become vulnerable over the long haul. If the foundation for such programs is not institutionalized and made a permanent part of the way work is done, the programs may not persist past the first few improvement projects.

Here are some steps to take to put the necessary organizational elements in place in order to position the business renovation activities for long-term continuation:

✓ **Select an Executive Sponsor**—The senior executive team is ultimately responsible for the success of ongoing business renovation. Specifically, a C-level leader must be designated as the executive sponsor of the business renovation function. As sponsor, the leader has the executive-level responsibility to impel the program forward and ensure its institutionalization. It is the sponsor's job to devise the means to properly staff and fund the function and determine strategies to overcome inherent resistances and garner support to safeguard success.

✓ **Institute a Business Renovation Center of Excellence (CoE)**— Considered a shared services unit, the center of excellence provides the horsepower needed to drive the transformation initiatives. It brings skilled practitioners, standard processes and automated tools to business renovation work. The organization reports directly to the executive sponsor in its infancy. However, it can be migrated to an existing shared services division, if one exists, once the CoE is stable.

✓ **Assign a Leader to the CoE**—This person is charged with the day-to-day management of the business renovation CoE. A senior executive in his or her own right, this C-level designee works with the executive sponsor to preach the gospel of business transformation across the enterprise by providing what is essential for the transformation initiatives to flourish.

✓ **Staff the CoE with Transformation Specialists** –Members of the CoE, these professionals are the "thought leaders" of the business renovation program. They can hail from both inside (staff member) and outside (consultant) the organization. Naturally, they come to the table with a rich and diverse experience in business optimization, and are usually experts in one or more of the continuous process improvement approaches, like Lean, Six Sigma, or TQM. Inevitably, they are responsible for modeling and analyzing business processes and developing the recommendations for change within each project.

✓ **Establish the Business Contract** –The business contract is an implicit understanding that exists between members of the CoE and management and staff from the business areas with whom they work. Put simply, the contract calls for active participation from business professionals on each transformation project. After all, who knows more about the business than those who do the work every day? These experts must be part of the effort to recast and redesign the business of the enterprise. The contract is established at the project level, and is enforced among the senior executive team.

These roles and organizational devices outlined above can be thought of as the foundation stones on which continuous transformation is built. They are essential elements for the long-term sustainability of business renovation activities. We should consider weaving them into our renovation program planning. See *Cummins Makes Transformation Work*, for an example from industry.

See It in Action

Cummins Makes Transformation Work

Cummins, Inc. is a global power leader that designs, manufactures, sells, and services diesel engines and related technology around the world. Headquartered in Columbus, Indiana, Cummins employs nearly 46,000 people worldwide and serves customers in over 190 countries. It generated over $17 billion in sales last year and looks to grow further in years to come.

It is an understatement to suggest that Cummins customer service operates in a complex landscape. With over 100 different contact centers, it can be difficult for customers to find the right person to respond to their inquiries. Therefore, the company decided to do something about it—launch a transformation program focused on contact centers as a way to improve the customer experience and reduce operational expenses.

Sponsored through the Office of the Chief Operating Officer, the initiative is staffed with highly experienced employees, including:

✓ **Program Leader**—with deep knowledge of Cummins businesses and customers,
✓ **Operations Leader**—with vast experience managing large contact centers across industries,
✓ **Technology Leader**—with experience delivering customer-facing technologies including telephony and CRM,
✓ **Business Process Leader**—with a background performing large-scale, process re-design projects.

The goal of the program is simple—resolve a customer's inquiry on first contact. By rethinking workflow and organizational design, the program also intends to set the enterprise standards for Cummins contact centers, develop a world-class workforce, and, ultimately, create a culture that engraves passion for customer service into the DNA of the entire organization.

The program is still evolving. However early indications are that it is having a major impact, with:

✓ increases of more than 40 percent in average speed of answer;
✓ reductions in average call handle time;
✓ reductions in abandoned calls;
✓ reductions in problem-resolution cycle time;
✓ increases of 22 percent in the firm's customer satisfaction index;

In the words of Dana Miller, director, Strategy and Business Processes at Cummins and a key member of the transformation effort:

"The customer experience formally became a critical, cross-business unit initiative under the Customer Support Excellence transformation

program at Cummins…It regularly reminds all of us to put the customer first, and provide real value in everything we do."

By putting people behind the transformation program, the Cummins approach serves as the global template for any business renovation initiative. It is how to make transformation work.

TO CLOSE

Re-imagining the way work is performed, utilizing human resources most efficiently, and exploring how to better leverage technologies are critically important to the ongoing success and evolution of our organizations. To become and remain "of Choice" demands a degree of swiftness in execution and rapid response to customer requirements that can only be achieved through rethinking and optimizing the way work is performed. Modern-day economic and technological trends only serve to accentuate the point.

However, change for the sake of change is not the best way to leverage precious resources to competitive gain. Rather, emphasis must be placed on architecting expansive business renovation programs that can aggressively transform an enterprise into one that will last for years to come. It is hoped that the checkpoints offered here will help your organization in its quest for enduring success.

We will look at the role technology and automation play in the next chapter.

7

ALIGN TECHNOLOGY—IT'S AT THE CORE OF ALL WE DO

One of the things that I've used on the Google is to pull up maps.
—George W. Bush

For the past two decades, computer gurus have predicted that computing technology will become so ubiquitous that it will one day be consumed as a utility, just like electricity and telephone service. That day is quickly coming upon us—made possible by advances in the Internet and mobile computing devices, and all of their related offshoots and requisite supporting substructures. Pardon the pun, but in this day and age we can virtually plug in and go!

Therefore, it is time for executives to stop being intimidated by technology discussions and, instead, establish a foundation for understanding the basic constructs that are reshaping the ways in which organizations process information and conduct business. In this way, we can drive the information technology (IT) strategies that will enable the dynamic business evolution so critical to remaining vital and competitive.

When followed, the checklist provided on the next page will demystify some of the most important technology concepts and offer a way for us to integrate them into our core strategies.

Technology Integration Checklist

✓ Define Where Technology Fits
✓ Know What You Have
✓ Learn What Is Available
✓ Separate Table Stakes from Competitive Advantages
✓ Mind the Gap to Reimagine the Future
✓ Weave Fresh Thinking into the Plan
✓ Monitor Technological Evolution

Let's explore these thoughts and learn how to apply them in the advancement of our organization's core strategies.

CHECKLIST ITEM 1: DEFINE WHERE TECHNOLOGY FITS

In order to drive the technology discussion within an organization, executives must first review all of the possible technological implications of their strategies. It is not enough to intimately know the organization's vision story. Indeed, we must be able to discern what role we are expecting technology to play within all of the projects and programs that comprise the enterprise's strategic plan. With this understanding, we can establish the linkages necessary to inform technology direction-setting.

A quick review of the projects and programs is all that is needed to gain the necessary perspective. Typically, the documentation used to describe the projects and programs includes a section that calls out the technology required by each initiative. This provides the first clue about the organization's technological expectations. However, it is wise to dig deeper because the documentation standard used may not specifically cover the technological implications of each initiative, and sometimes there are additional implications that are not explicitly defined.

Here is a list of technological implications that came from a few of my recent clients' strategic planning efforts. It is indicative of the ways in which technology requirements can be buried within the details of a strategic plan:

✓ **Claims Adjudication Process Redesign Project**: A major property and casualty insurer exposed the need for developing a mobile computing application as a means to support the newly reengineered business process;

✓ **Service Delivery Project**: A country-wide retailer identified the requirement to build an online customer support portal;

✓ **Sales Improvement Project**: A global manufacturer determined the provision of a Web-based sales support product as a condition of project completion;

✓ **Customer Intimacy Project**: A regional financial services firm called for the acquisition of a cloud-based Customer Relationship Management (CRM) package as prerequisite to the completion of its "Customer First" initiative;

✓ **Product Distribution Project**: A niche software company recognized that the best solution for it to remain competitive involved retooling its packaged software products into a Software-as-a- Service (SaaS) solution.

It is important to recognize all of the technology implications of our strategies because it is the only way that we can be sure that nothing falls through the cracks and negatively impacts our enterprise's long-term success.

For additional emphasis, it is wise to establish a set of technology-oriented business principles as a means to ensure that management's preferences for technology deployment are integrated into the way IT work is done. Technology principles define the "rules of the road" for IT practices within a concern. For an example, see *FDIC's Technology Principles*.

See It in Action

FDIC's Technology Principles

The recent financial crisis brought enormous pressure to the Federal Deposit Insurance Corporation (FDIC), one of the US government's banking industry watchdogs, to step up its efforts to identify and monitor troubled banks, close failed banks, and manage receiverships to the benefit of depositors and the insurance fund.

As a result, new regulatory requirements emerged that obliged the FDIC to expand its workforce and revamp its IT infrastructure so as to accommodate the necessary organizational and operational changes. In an effort to ensure proper technology and business alignment during these troubled times, the FDIC adopted the following 16 technology principles:

1. FDIC business needs drive FDIC IT decisions;
2. Business process reengineering and improvements will typically precede implementation of new technology;
3. Information technology must be adaptable to meet changing business needs and the business environment in which the FDIC operates;
4. Information technology must be accessible to individuals (both members of the public and FDIC staff and contractors) with disabilities in accordance with Section 508;
5. Architecture promotes the integration of business processes and provides a common operating environment;
6. Data is a FDIC asset that should be managed from a corporate perspective;
7. Data is accessible, reliable, and of a high quality;
8. Applications should be partitioned to separate presentation, business logic and data;
9. Applications shall be infrastructure independent to facilitate scalability and adaptability;
10. Applications shall reuse existing capabilities, services, and components;
11. Application are modular to facilitate maintainability and built for high availability;
12. Infrastructure is managed as a service that can respond to demands for infrastructure components or capacity changes in a fast, efficient manner;

13. The FDIC infrastructure is reliable, available, and recoverable;

14. The FDIC will limit complexity of the infrastructure;

15. Access to IT resources will be controlled and limited to those with legitimate business needs; and

16. Applications are developed and designed to be secure.

These technology principles are actively applied whenever new IT initiatives are being considered for inclusion in the FDIC strategic plan and whenever new technology is being developed in support of existing agency initiatives. These principles serve as a great example of what an organization can do in order to ensure the appropriate integration of technology and strategy.

Source: "Federal Deposit Insurance Corporation: Business Technology Strategic Plan 2013–2017," FDIC, January 24, 2013, p. 17.

CHECKLIST ITEM 2: KNOW WHAT YOU HAVE

With a better understanding of where technology fits within the strategic vision, it is wise to create a baseline inventory of the organization's existing IT architecture. A baseline audit of the computing environment is needed in order to assess how well the enterprise is technologically positioned to support its plans for the future.

Some organizations have such an IT baseline readily available, while others do not. Its existence seems to depend on several factors, including the size, years in business, number of physical locations, and level of sophistication of IT personnel within the enterprise. If your organization does not have a current IT baseline, it will be necessary to staff and fund a strategic project to deliver one.

When working with clients on this, I prefer to organize the IT baseline across these four dimensions:

✓ **Workplace:** The Workplace Dimension of the IT baseline captures characteristics about the way in which work is currently performed within the enterprise. The organizational design, business functions, worker types, and work locations are all identified and cross-referenced against the information, applications, and technology that are used in the workplace.

✓ **Information:** The Information Dimension of the IT baseline collects and presents particulars about the data used in support of the organization. Details about the type, source, locale, and volume of the data are charted against the other three dimensions of the IT baseline so as to ascertain how information is managed within the enterprise.

✓ **Application:** The Application Dimension of the IT baseline contains the current systems portfolio that is in place within the concern. Key features and functions of each application are defined and mapped against the Workplace, Information, and Technology views of the IT baseline.

✓ **Technology:** The Technology Dimension of the IT baseline documents the current hardware inventories, standards, configurations, usage statistics, and processing capacities of the boxes and pipes that support the enterprise. This view of the IT baseline is plotted against the others to present a clear picture of the organization's computing environment.

We can better plan the future course of technology deployment within our organizations by knowing the intersection points of these four views of the computing environment. Check out *Jump-starting an IT Baseline Effort*, for a sampling of the kinds of questions to ask when beginning a new IT baseline initiative.

See It in Action

Jump-starting an IT Baseline Effort

It can be a daunting task to initiate an IT baseline project. There is just so much ground to cover. Where do you start?

I have found that it is a good idea to have a small set of open-ended questions at my fingertips in order to jump-start the effort. Here is a sampling of them, organized along the four dimensions of IT baseline work outlined in this chapter:

Workplace Dimension Questions:

✓ What work is done within the enterprise?
✓ Who does the work?
✓ How is the work performed?
✓ When is the work accomplished?
✓ Where is it executed?

Information Dimension Questions:

✓ What information is currently used by the business?
✓ How much information is available?
✓ What form does it take?
✓ Where is it needed?
✓ How often is it refreshed?

Application Dimension Questions:

✓ What automated systems are in use today?
✓ What information does each system manipulate?
✓ Where do the applications reside?
✓ Where are they used?
✓ When are they used?

Technology Dimension Questions:

✓ What technology is in place today?
✓ How is it used?
✓ Who uses it?
✓ Where does the technology reside?
✓ When was it last upgraded?

The answers to these basic questions, along with any additional qualifying ones, help to paint a clearer picture of the current workplace, information, application, and technology environments that exist within the organization. This IT baseline is an important element of assessing how well situated an enterprise is in meeting its long-term business vision.

CHECKLIST ITEM 3: LEARN WHAT IS AVAILABLE

With an understanding and assessment of the existing technology within the concern readily available via the IT baseline work, an executive team must familiarize itself with the emerging technological trends that are reshaping business strategies. Unquestionably, there is a fear among business executives of being unable to grasp seemingly sophisticated topics. However, leaving it only to the IT professionals to figure out is just shirking our responsibility. Here are a few IT trends worth learning about. They are, and will continue to be, factors that influence strategic thinking over the next few years:

✓ **Internet of Things:** Everyday items are embedded with computer devices that can be connected and fully integrated with the Web. Some examples include wireless sensor networks used in smart home monitoring, radio-frequency-identification-tagged consumer goods used in inventory control and real-time camera feeds from stop lights involved in traffic flow management. The physical world is quickly becoming system enabled, allowing it to be fused with the digital world. Executives should consider the implications for this trend on their organizations.

✓ **Mobile Computing:** From tablets to smart phones, people are increasingly relying on their mobile devices to assist them in managing their lives. Businesses are already building apps that accommodate the needs of their mobile-minded customers. The next phase of evolution will demand computer device independence, enabling an uninterrupted computing experience as we move from device to device throughout our daily lives. How will the organizations that we are responsible for adapt to the continued evolution of mobile computing?

✓ **Cloud Computing:** There is a variety of cloud computing solutions available, including:

- *Software as a Service* (SaaS)—SaaS is a software distribution model in which automated systems are hosted by a service provider and made available to customers over a network. The SaaS vendor is responsible for upgrades and troubleshooting, and commonly provides the infrastructure and backup/recovery capabilities as well.

- *Infrastructure as a Service* (IaaS)—Data storage, hardware, servers, and networking equipment are provided to the customer on a per-use basis by the IaaS vendor, who holds the equipment and is responsible for housing, running, and maintaining it.

- *Platform as a Service* (PaaS)—PaaS is a service delivery model that provides the capability to lease the hardware, operating systems, storage, and network capacity over the Internet. It allows customers to rent virtualized servers and associated services needed to develop, test, and run applications.

- *Business Process as a Service* (BPaaS)—Procurement, payment processing, and payroll are just a few of the business functions that can be supported through BPaaS vendors, who provide the necessary infrastructure so that organizations no longer need to staff and perform the activities in-house.

Cloud computing has the potential to dramatically change the way organizations use computer technology, replacing the need to buy and maintain computing systems and hardware with a much more cost-effective, on-demand model, similar in nature to the ways in which utilities provide water and electricity to their customers.

✓ **Social Media**: There's no doubt that social media is here to stay. Social networks like Facebook, Twitter, and LinkedIn manage communities comprised of millions of people worldwide. Social media is too big to ignore. The challenge for most enterprises is determining how to best harness the potential. As executives, we must devise strategies that allow our organizations to leverage social media in order to optimize our presence, generate product and brand awareness, enhance employee engagement, improve customer relations, augment product/service development, and supplement staffing efforts.

✓ **Gamification**: Gamification refers to the use of game thinking and mechanics in software design in order to improve the ways in which automated applications are used and the methods by which people engage with technology. Most organizations intend to leverage gamification for the purposes of marketing, customer retention, productivity measurement, and training. We are already seeing firms like American Express, Hertz, and Starbucks use it as underpinnings to their latest loyalty programs. We will need to get a handle on this trend in order to manage it for competitive gain (For more on the subject, please see *Gamification Hits the Big Time*).

While submergence into the subject of IT can be intimidating for some executives, a rudimentary understanding of evolving developments, like the ones outlined above, is an essential responsibility of all senior leadership. After all, a limited knowledge of the possibilities will only limit your organization's ability to remain vital and strong.

See It in Action

Gamification Hits the Big Time

A recent report from the Gartner Group, a well-respected IT Industry analysis firm, concludes:

"By 2014, a gamified service for consumer goods marketing and customer retention will become as important as Facebook, eBay or Amazon, and more than 70% of Global 2000 organizations will have at least one gamified application."[1]

With such a claim, it is clear that gamification has hit the big time. Here are a few examples of how some early adopters are already using the technology:

✓ **Domino's Pizza:** The restaurant's *Pizza Hero* mobile app allows customers to place their order for delivery while applying for a job at their local Domino's location.

✓ **Microsoft:** *Ribbon Hero 2.0* is the software giant's game that helps new customers get up to speed with all of the rich features and functions of the Microsoft Office suite. Users can earn points and track their progress through leaderboards that further engagement and enhance learning.

✓ **Nike:** The *NikeFuel* app tracks and monitors players progress through a series of "missions," all fueled by a players everyday movements. Each mission begins with advice from a Nike athlete, like Calvin Johnson or Alex Morgan, suggesting the use of innovative Nike products that will enable a player's successful graduation to the next game level.

✓ **Playboy:** The publisher's *"Miss Social"* app created a competition in which fans submitted their photos for a chance to be "Miss Social." Playboy estimates that their online revenue grew by 60 percent and raised their number of active users to over 80,000.

✓ **US Army:** The *America's Army* game was developed by the US Army to attract potential recruits. It has proven to be a cost-effective enlistment strategy, as millions of registered users have been brought to the attention of the military through the use of the game.

These are just a few examples of how organizations are weaving gamification into their strategies in order to recruit like-minded individuals, enhance customer loyalty, and grow revenue. How gamification will be used in our organizations is up to us. However, we must get on the bandwagon or be left in the dust.

CHECKLIST ITEM 4: SEPARATE TABLES STAKES FROM COMPETITIVE ADVANTAGE

As described in the introduction to this chapter, we are entering an age in which computing capabilities are being offered as a consumable commodity. Enabled through the widespread use of portable devices and availability of myriad cloud computing options, an on-demand, pay-as-you-go service model for IT is readily available for any organization to use.

Has the playing field been leveled? After all, computing innovation and horsepower are no longer strategic differentiators, when they can be acquired at will. However, here is where we as executive leaders must challenge conventional wisdom. There is quite a difference between fielding core business applications that support back office functions like administrative support, accounting, and payroll and developing automated capabilities that drive product leadership, operational superiority, and customer allegiance (Take a look at what one company is doing to redefine the rules of the food service industry in *Golden State Foods Delivers through the Cloud*).

Therefore, our challenge lies in the ability to separate those computing capabilities that are absolutely needed just to stay in the game (that is, "table stakes") from the novel application of those same capabilities in ways that lead to a competitive advantage. Innovation is born in the ability to do the latter.

Here are some examples of how existing computing technology capabilities are being used in innovative ways in order to differentiate:

✓ **Product Leadership:** Nike, Ford, and Apple are embedding computing devices and using apps to improve the features and functions of their products. You can track your workouts, find your misplaced iPhone, and reroute your commute using their products;

✓ **Operational Superiority:** UPS, Walmart, and The Home Depot are using cloud computing capabilities to optimize delivery routing, restructure purchasing agreements, and streamline supply chain management into best-of-breed processes;

✓ **Customer Allegiance:** Amazon and Netflix use cloud-based CRM capabilities to expose their patrons to specific products that may interest them and distribute those products in the format, and through the delivery channel, defined by their customers.

Indeed, computing technology can be consumed as needed. However, the best enterprises can redefine the terms and drive innovation by applying technology in new and exciting ways—just like the best organizations did when IT was still in its infancy.

See It in Action

Golden State Foods Delivers through the Cloud

Claiming such industry leaders as Arby's, Denny's, KFC, McDonalds, Pizza Hut, and Starbucks as customers, Golden State Foods (GSF) is one of the largest diversified suppliers in the food service industry. It supplies all kinds of items, including meat, produce, condiments, sauces, and baked goods, to major fast food restaurants. In total, GSF services more than 20,000 restaurants in over 50 countries around the world. It is growing in leaps and bounds due in part to its "*When customers succeed, we succeed*" philosophy.

The Irvine, California-based company employs over 4,000 people. It uses a decentralized business model to support its distribution and food processing operations within the United States. Due to tremendous growth and customer demand, GSF had spawned 27 mini-data centers around the country. It became increasingly difficult for the technology department to keep up.

Further, the decentralized IT environment was difficult to manage, lacked needed elasticity to support the ebb and flow of the business, and its hardware footprint had tremendous redundancy across its data centers, making it extremely expensive to maintain and inordinately slow to extend when needed.

The firm decided to consolidate and centralize its IT infrastructure by migrating to a "pay-as-you-go" cloud computing model. It used a combination of SaaS and PaaS solutions to "right-size" its cloud so that it could optimally support the company's major business applications, office suites, and email systems.

With the help of Computer Sciences Corporation (CSC), GSF established private clouds at a primary data center in Newark, Delaware, and a secondary data center in Chicago, Illinois. With CSC as service provider, GSF simply consumes computing resources as it would any other utility, a model that provides needed agility while helping seamlessly integrate IT with the business.

Accordingly, technology deployment is delivered with greater speed, flexibility, and reliability, allowing it to be viewed by the executive team as strategic enabler that is available as needed to deliver top-tier customer support—that will differentiate GSF in the marketplace, and thereby contribute to more business growth and revenue generation.

As GSF's chief information officer, Rhonda Sias, explains:

"We can get a new distribution center up and running in a matter of weeks rather than three to five months, eliminating that bottleneck is good for business all around. If we can quickly launch a new Starbucks distribution center that can start servicing another 150 stores, that helps our customers grow, which helps us grow."[2]

It also helps to redefine a new normal for the food service industry and remind us, as executives, that it is our job to seek out technology alternatives that can help us to drive product leadership, operational superiority, and customer allegiance.

Source: "Success Story: Golden State Foods," Computer Sciences Corporation, February 17, 2012.

CHECKLIST ITEM 5: MIND THE GAPS TO REIMAGINE THE FUTURE

With a better grasp of what our organizations already have at hand from a computing standpoint, and a fuller understanding of what is available, it is time to redefine where we want to go. In light of the possibilities that advancing computing capabilities have to offer, there can be gaps between what is in the plan and what should be there. Minding the gaps to reimagine the future is an important step to take in order to ensure that the strategic plan is always all that it can be.

Fueled by the latest advances in computing, old-fashioned rules about an enterprise's fixed and variable costs are being tested. Organizations are already beginning to forgo mass, in favor of establishing more *"mutable"* business structures that can scale to size and capacity as desired. This allows enterprises to compete on a more variable cost basis, while enhancing the suppleness needed for rapid response to evolving customer desires and global market demands (see **Transforming Fujitsu's UK through Innovative IT Delivery**, for an example).

See It in Action

Transforming Fujitsu's UK through Innovative IT Delivery

Fujitsu is a leading provider of IT services and products. It employs 14,000 people in the United Kingdom and Ireland and generates annual revenues of £2 billion. Driven by the desire to establish an integrated IT infrastructure that could support the recently merged Fujitsu companies in the United Kingdom and Ireland, the firm decided to pursue a more flexible solution—one that could flex up when workloads demanded more computing capabilities and adjust downward during slower periods so as to reduce costs and establish a smaller carbon footprint.

A project team was formed to review the situation and determine how best to proceed. It immediately looked to the IaaS concept as a means to host its business applications on a shared infrastructure with all of the necessary levels of security, resilience, and performance features designed in.

When presenting his team's recommendations, Sean Barker, the team's project manager, used this analogy to win over the Fujitsu UK senior executive team:

"Think of it in terms of vehicles. Previously, everyone had their own car which for most of the time was left unused in the car park. But with a car pool system we would need far fewer vehicles in total and whenever I need a car, I take it from the pool and not only that, I can choose a large or small car depending on my needs. That's how IaaS works—instead of owning IT, use what you want when you want it. That means a much improved utilization and lower costs for those workloads where dedicated IT is not needed all the time."[3]

Barker's team was absolutely correct in its thinking. The firm's IaaS strategy is already paying significant dividends, including

✓ **Reduced Capital Expenditures**—Fujitsu saved £3M by using IaaS instead of buying new servers and storage systems;

✓ **Lower Operating Costs**—hosting costs reduced by 20 percent;

✓ **Diminished Cost of Ownership**—as the IT infrastructure can decrease as required, the cost is eliminated when the technology is no longer needed;

✓ **Quicker Business Response**—additional server and storage capacity, available in hours rather than months for faster business project implementations;

✓ **Improved Convenience**—since technology refreshes by design, obsolescence challenges of the past have been eliminated;

✓ **Enriched Environmental Impact**—using IaaS means that the server utilization will increase from 10 percent to 70 percent on average, enabling approximately 85 percent energy and carbon saving.

Soon, the type of innovative approach employed by Fujitsu UK will become more the norm than the exception. Until then, it serves as a wonderful example of how businesses can deliver IT in ways that lower costs and enhance agility.

Source: "*CASE STUDY: Infrastructure-as-a-Service Transforms Fujitsu's UK Operations*," Fujitsu Limited, http://www.fujitsu.com/uk/Images/fujitsu-iaas.pdf, September 2010.

Periodically, we need to revisit our vision stories and ensure that our vision is expansive enough to accommodate the possibilities that are enabled through ongoing computing advances. Considering only the examples provided earlier in the chapter, some adjustments in strategic thinking may involve

✓ using the Internet of Things and embedded computing concepts to differentiate product and service offerings;

✓ using mobile computing concepts to enable physical independence strategies;

✓ using SaaS as a cost-effective way to enable application refresh strategies;

✓ using PaaS as a cost-effective way to enable technology refresh strategies;

✓ using IaaS as a means to lower operating expenses and improve scalability;

✓ using BPaaS as a means to virtually outsource routine business functions;

✓ using social media to manage the brand and assist in product launch strategies;

✓ using gamification capabilities in customer loyalty campaigns.

Indeed, by regularly minding the gaps between current thinking and the world of possibilities made available through newly emerging technological capabilities can keep our strategic thinking fresh and pure.

CHECKLIST ITEM 6: WEAVE FRESH THINKING INTO THE PLAN

As strategic visions are refreshed, it is important to translate the new thinking into projects and programs for inclusion in the strategic plan. As described in Chapter 3, all existing "gaps" should be plugged through the identification of new initiatives. It is the executive's job to tie up the loose ends that can result from ongoing technology examination activities by feeding the strategic planning process with additional business opportunities as required.

Described another way, if we discover that a new technology should be acquired or an advanced computing approach must be exploited as part of a new strategy, then it is crucial that we document that fact as a new initiative, determine its priority, and incorporate the effort into our organization's strategic plan. This is the way in which we can weave fresh thinking into the plan—seamlessly integrating technology into what we do as an enterprise. See *An Epic Mix of Technology at Vail Resorts*, for an example.

See It in Action

An Epic Mix of Technology at Vail Resorts

It began with the modest quest of making life simpler for the guests and providing a trouble-free experience that would keep them coming back for more. That is why the resort's management team began to embed radio frequency (RF) technology into its lift tickets and guest passes—so visitors wouldn't have to fumble around searching for their ski pass each time they wanted to use a lift. It morphed into something bigger once the firm decided that it needed to reassess its marketing strategies in light of the rising popularity of social media channels like Facebook and Twitter.

Understanding that RF technology could be leveraged to capture all kinds of facts and figures about each skier's day on the slopes, and that social media could be used as a way for guests to share such information as lifts ridden, runs per day, and vertical feet skied, Vail Resorts decided to build EpicMix, an online portal and corresponding mobile app that enables visitors to easily share their tales and triumphs about their time on the mountain with friends and family alike.

To make the experience even more compelling, the management team extended the application's capabilities by introducing a gamification component that serves to track guests' activities and reward them with electronic badges for their accomplishments.

EpicMix became a colossal hit among resortgoers in its first season, with:

- ✓ approximately 40 percent of all guests downloading the mobile apps;
- ✓ nearly 100,000 guests activating an account;
- ✓ over 6 million e-badges awarded;
- ✓ approximately 45,000 skiers sharing accomplishments on Facebook and Twitter;
- ✓ the generating of more than 35 million social impressions.

In the words of Darren Jacoby, director of Customer Relationship Marketing at Vail Resorts:

"We could never have imagined the passion EpicMix would evoke from our guests. We can truly say that EpicMix delivers the experience of a lifetime."[4]

It is unmistakable that the executive team at Vail Resorts struck gold with its EpicMix portal implementation. The initiative extended existing customer experience strategies (that is, RF-embedded lift tickets) into other strategies that achieved even higher degrees of customer loyalty by folding social media and gamification into the mix.

EpicMix is an outstanding illustration of what can be done when leaders take the time to review existing strategies, identify gaps in current approaches, and weave fresh ideas and thinking into their organization's strategic plans.

Source: "*Vail Resorts Creates Epic Experiences with Customer Intelligence,*," SAS Institute, Inc., July 26, 2012, pp. 4–6.

CHECKLIST ITEM 7: MONITOR TECHNOLOGICAL EVOLUTION

Computing technology will never stop evolving. Thus, it is imperative that we put in place a means of monitoring technological evolution. The monitoring approach adopted must accommodate the regular review of both the technological progress made within our organizations and the external advancement of computing capabilities available in the marketplace. In this way, we can warrant that our enterprises are always staying on top of the technological trends that may influence ongoing success.

Among the senior management team, IT leaders are likely to be best suited for monitoring technological evolution—inside and out. Their role and contribution to strategic direction-setting has been growing over the years. It would seem that charging them with the responsibility for deliberately tracking and regularly reporting on technology evolution represents the next logical step on the IT leadership maturity curve.

What's more, since IT use is becoming commodity, leaders responsible for technology management are pressured to be less technical and more skilled in contract negotiation and vendor management. Therefore, the monitoring of trends and advancing capabilities provides them with additional insight that can be applied in these newer roles.

It should be noted that in many ways, placing the technology monitoring responsibility within the IT function is not a huge departure from what some concerns already have instituted. However, formalizing the monitoring process and tying it to strategy-setting means that the information gathered and shared from the process can be better targeted for use in strategic planning.

In essence, keeping track of, and "dummying down," technical information and trends enables better understanding. Further, it positions computing discussions to become more mainstream within the C-level suite and less intimidating for the *technophobes* among the executive rank, which, as discussed at the outset of the chapter, is immediately essential for qualifying senior leaders to continue to ably steer the ship.

TO CLOSE

It is critical to note that the technology decisions made today are indispensably central to the long-term health of the enterprise. Accordingly, executives must stop conceding technology decision-making responsibility to technologists and begin to expand their own awareness and understanding of the possibilities that today's technologies enable, so that they can devise strategies to better exploit these and future technological capabilities required to fulfill their organization's strategic vision.

Subsequently, whether to use cloud computing or push the limits of gamification isn't the point. These concepts, as well as their underlying infrastructures, will continue to grow, mature, and change over time. However, it is essential to recognize that computing technology must be seamlessly integrated into all that we do. The specific approaches used to achieve this seamless integration are our choices to make as executive leaders. These are the same choices that will determine lasting success. Hence, we must choose wisely.

8

TRANSFORM STAFF—THE PEOPLE PART OF ENTERPRISE-WIDE CHANGE

Things do not change; we change.

—Henry David Thoreau

Every organization is comprised of people (staff) who are doing work (process) and using tools (technology) to get the work done. Thus far, we've explored the process and technology implications of managing enterprise-wide change. Now, it is time to look at what we can do to help our staff members transform, so that they can be more effective and better aligned with an ever-changing organization.

Training, measurement, and reward are three pillars on which the platform for staff transformation is shaped. Each of these pillars is equally important and mutually supporting of the other. If one of the pillars is weak, the transformation effort can tumble; if one of the pillars rises past the others, the whole change process can be jeopardized.

To ensure ultimate success, it is essential that the training, measurement, and reward programs of the enterprise be well organized and coordinated in a deliberate fashion. Review the following checklist items to be certain that all of the finer points of each of the three programs are understood and appropriately covered within your organization.

Staff Transformation Checklist

✓ Shape the Program for Continuous Execution
✓ Place Emphasis on Softer Skills and Bigger Pictures
✓ Commit to Shared Training
✓ Weave Measurement into the Execution Environment
✓ Measure for Desired Outcomes
✓ Reward Results
✓ Reimagine Incentives
✓ Build a Creative Team of Personnel

Let's initiate our exploration of these staff transformation checklist items by evoking the importance of synchronizing the training, measurement, and reward processes within an enterprise. To reiterate, the three must work in harmony in order to successfully transform our people.

CHECKLIST ITEM 1: SHAPE THE PROGRAM FOR CONTINUOUS EXECUTION

As mentioned at the outset of the chapter, a staff transformation program rests upon the three pillars of training, measurement, and reward. Because of the interdependencies that exist among these three organizational elements, we can consider the program to drive staff transformation to be both cyclical and continuous. Like any transformative program, staff transformation is never really finished. Rather, it changes, grows, and continues over time.

Training starts the cycle. We train for the skills and behaviors that are called out in our vision and business strategies. Once staff are properly trained, execution proceeds and the measurement part of the staff transformation cycle begins. As results are measured and outcomes determined, the reward phase of the cycle is triggered and performed. The cycle continues onward, constantly evolving as the organization progresses towards its vision.

Because of these dynamics, it is important to shape the program for continuous execution. Done well, the training, measurement, and reward processes that we have in place today will prepare our organizations for tomorrow. However, once there, these approaches to the three pillars of staff transformation will no longer suffice. In effect, they'll be yesterday's news. Therefore, we must be sure to design the program in a way that regularly introduces fresh and complementary methods to the mix across all three of its dimensions. See *Commissioning a Staff Transformation Program*, for an example of a program brief that was developed for a client who wanted to kick-off a project to construct its staff transformation program.

See It in Action

Commissioning a Staff Transformation Program

A program brief is a device that I use in my consulting practice to concisely capture the intention of a new initiative that is being evaluated by executive management for possible inclusion in a client's strategic plan.

The following program brief was used to document a Staff Transformation Program initiative idea that they had identified:

Project Name: Staff Transformation Program Planning Project

Description: This project is intended to establish a Staff Transformation Program Plan. The program plan will be used to integrate the training, measurement, and reward systems within the company. All of the specific initiatives required to align and execute these related processes will be maintained within the program plan. The program will evolve over time in order to stay in sync with company direction and evolving strategies.

Objectives:

✓ to better align staff with the company's strategic vision through skills and behavior transformation;

✓ to improve business performance through enhanced staff capabilities;

✓ to enhance workforce productivity and job satisfaction through the provision of improved training, measurement, and reward systems;

✓ to engage staff in the process of change; and

✓ to be an employer of choice in the business communities in which we operate by creating a rich and varied work environment.

Work Products:

✓ a multi-year Staff Transformation Program Plan;

✓ a set of project and programs briefs, in priority order and spread across the planning timeline, that summarizes each initiative to be included in the plan;

✓ a list of "Quick Hit" initiatives that could be implemented immediately as a means of establishing momentum and building "good faith" across the company;

✓ a recommendation for maintaining the program plan as it evolves.

Resource Estimate: A cross-functional team of 6–8 members for 3 days per week for 8 weeks

Project Timeline: January 3, 2011 to February 25, 2011

The company successfully implemented the program planning project as outlined above, and is in the midst of executing on the various initiatives that make up the program. For our purposes, the brief nicely summarizes the intention of a Staff Transformation program.

CHECKLIST ITEM 2: PLACE EMPHASIS ON SOFTER SKILLS AND BIGGER PICTURES

Most organizations provide some level of training to their personnel, if no more than on-the-job. However, training efforts are largely job specific. Standard training programs teach people how to inspect a part, stock a shelf, perform an audit, and so forth. However, few training programs do an exceptional job at preparing staff to contribute beyond the performance of their daily work function. This needs to change.

We must place an emphasis on soft skills development and on presenting a bigger picture for our staff members. Soft skills help people to think more broadly about what their work is all about. Training focused on enhancing communication, building trust, and promoting teamwork, for example, fosters collaboration, cooperation, and esprit de corps. A workforce comprised of personnel who support each other and work as one can produce incredible results.

What's more, using training as a means to present a bigger picture to the staff of what the enterprise is all about and what it is attempting to accomplish helps them to think beyond their specific job. By the organization's raising awareness of the whole job (see Chapter 6), workers gain a broader perspective of the work of the enterprise. This improves their ability to anticipate and properly adjust to changes being made within the organization so as to remain properly aligned and positioned to aptly deliver.

Further, a deeper appreciation of the enterprise's vision and strategies also provides benefit to the organization. Personnel are better positioned to offer improvement ideas and suggest meaningful changes in the operation, once they develop a broader perspective of the organization's strategic goals and direction. See *Transforming Talent at Whirlpool*, for an illustration of the concept in action.

See It in Action

Transforming Talent at Whirlpool

Whirlpool Corporation, headquartered in Benton Harbor, Michigan, is a leader in the $120 billion global home appliance industry. Its appliances, with brand names that include *Whirlpool*, *Maytag*, *KitchenAid*, *Jenn-Air*, *Amana*, *Bauknecht*, *Brastemp*, and *Consul*, are marketed in nearly every country around the world.

Innovation is the main underpinning of Whirlpool Corporation's strategy. It is the only way for it to hold off the competition. Therefore, in a push to reinforce this notion, the company set about developing a training outreach program to its over 80,000 staff members. The centerpiece of the training program is a customized offering codeveloped with the American Management Association (AMA), a leading training and education company. It teaches staff how to think innovatively.

Consequently, with a deeper understanding of the company's strategic intentions, personnel have developed innovative thinking as a core competency. They are now better positioned to offer thoughts and suggestions for significant enhancements to the firm's products and services. Business processes have been redesigned, an innovation management system has been built, and the culture of the company has been changed for the good.

In fact, Whirlpool has earned many accolades for its high standards of operation and commendable work culture, including:

✓ **Fortune Magazine** ranked Whirlpool No. 1 in its 2011 World's Most Admired Companies® list in the Home Equipment, Furnishings industry;

✓ **Forbes Magazine** and Reputation Institute named Whirlpool one of the Top 25 Most Respected U.S. Companies for three consecutive years (2008–2011);

✓ **Fast Company Magazine** ranked Whirlpool No. 6 on its 2011 list of the World's Most Innovative Companies in the Consumer Products category;

✓ Whirlpool was named one of the **Best Employers** in Argentina and one of the **Best Companies to Work For** in Brazil (1997–2010), India and Mexico;

✓ The company has also been honored with 23 ENERGY STAR awards overall, more than any other appliance manufacturer.

Whirlpool's commitment to "big picture" training sets it apart from many of its competitors. It is that same commitment that has contributed to the firm's being held in such high regard by industry wonks and staff, alike.

Source: *"Whirlpool: An AMA Corporate Learning Solutions Success Story,"* *American Management Association,* http://www.amanet.org/organizations/ Whirlpool.aspx

CHECKLIST ITEM 3: COMMIT TO SHARED TRAINING

Unquestionably, organizations must train their staffs. However, they can't singularly be responsible for providing *all* of the training and education that each employee needs. This is especially true in this day and age when job changes are frequent and the next generation of workers, Gen Y (see Chapter 4 for more on their work style and habits), prefer the independence and variety that comes with free agency.

Indeed, it would be foolhardy for an enterprise to spend millions of dollars to fully train staff that may not stick around long enough to deliver a pay back on the investment. Therefore, we must shift from company-provided training to shared training, a more equitable model in which the cost and responsibility of training are shared between organization and staff.

Shared training can take many forms. Classically, an enterprise provides a set curriculum of technical and soft skills training, while encouraging staff to pursue additional training in complementary skills that they want to develop. The organization may pay for some part of the extracurricular education or just allow the employee paid time to educate him- or herself.

Another variation is one in which the enterprise pays for the training and the employee covers time and / or travel. Tuition reimbursement is a common example of this concept in action. But it can apply more widely and include webinars, professional associations, conferences, and seminars. The point is that staff and organization alike have some skin in the game. It is likely that staff will take the training more seriously when they are committing their own time and / or money to acquire it.

Nevertheless, shared training models provide an employee the freedom to develop his or her own personalized development plan in support of his or her career goals, and it provides an organization with better qualified personnel over time, fashioning a corporate culture that is highly productive and readily attracts top talent (see ***UTC's Billion Dollar Program***, for an example of the concept in action).

See It in Action

UTC's Billion Dollar Program

On January 31, 2012, the National Association of Independent Colleges and Universities gave its annual award for promoting higher education to United Technologies. This is the first time the association's award has been given to a company. It prompted David L. Warren, president of the independent colleges association, to remark:

"We think it's a model for the nation, one that hopefully other corporations might follow."[1]

United Technologies Corporation (UTC), headquartered in Hartford, Connecticut, is a diversified company that provides a broad range of high technology products and services to the global aerospace and building systems industries. From jet engines manufactured by Pratt & Whitney to escalators built by Otis Elevators, UTC's more than 200,000 employees supply big-ticket products to customers around the globe. With net sales of over $57 billion in 2012, the company has broad reach and influence. It is no wonder that it has spent over $1 billion in staff education reimbursement since 1996. With more than 34,000 degrees earned, the firm's Employee Scholar Program is exemplary.

The UTC program pays 100 percent of the cost of tuition and books for any employee seeking an associate's, bachelor's, or graduate degree, as long as he or she maintains a 3.0 or better grade point average. There are no rules about what courses to take or degrees to pursue. That's up to the employee to decide. However, most studying must be done on an employee's own time—evenings and weekends.

This is a solid example of a shared training model practice that an organization can choose to adopt, one in which the cost and responsibility of training are shared between organization and staff. In the UTC program, staff members take the responsibility to seek out and invest their time in pursuit of the degree that they are interested in earning, while the firm funds the education effort.

Everybody wins when they have a shared stake in the training game!

Source: "A $1 Billion 'Model' Employee Education Program," by Steve Lohr, NY Times Bits Blog, January 31, 2012.

CHECKLIST ITEM 4: WEAVE MEASUREMENT INTO EXECUTION ENVIRONMENT

Gathering statistics, reporting results, and calculating performance measurements can be tedious, especially if done after the fact. Besides rendering management intervention next to impossible, performance measurement that is developed following the time that the work is performed reeks of overhead and is often fraught with error. Weaving measurement processes into the execution environment is an alternative worth considering.

When measurement is tightly wound within job execution, performance metrics are produced as a direct byproduct of doing the work. There is no postwork completion effort to determine job performance results. In fact, when fully integrated with job execution, subpar work can be identified as it is being performed—by both the worker and his or her management team.

This, just-in-time measurement, is useful in more ways than one. It not only notifies all involved that there may be a problem but it offers an opportunity for managers and staff to collaborate on the best corrective action to take in order and get results back on track.

Further, providing easier access to critical performance information will enhance decision-making and position the organization to fine-tune performance metrics for better strategic alignment over time.

However, there are some implications to consider when pursuing the idea, including:

✓ a business re-engineering process that analyzes core business practices must be performed to ensure that relevant and efficient work processes

are automated and that the automation includes a performance
tracking capability;

✓ a process for determining the evolving performance measurement
information needs within the organization should be established
to ensure that the "right" information is being captured for solid
decision-making;

✓ easy and flexible access to the performance measurement information
by both personnel and their management should be enabled through
automation. In this way, the workforce can make adjustments and
learn through experience tracking;

✓ software tools that allow users to query information databases on an
ad-hoc basis (and control the appearance of report contents) are an
important way to improve productivity. Therefore, reporting capabilities
should be included in the performance measurement toolset;

✓ executive information systems will need to be designed to provide senior
management with summary information and the ability to "drill down"
and display as much detail as needed for proper decision-making.

Indeed, performance measurement data tends to be summary information composed as a result of doing the work of the enterprise. It would
seem obvious that performance measurement automation could be placed
"on top" of the business-processing environment and be used to capture
and derive meaning from measurements gathered on the spot. This would
eliminate the need to complete a separate set of activities in order to derive
performance results. As implied, it also establishes a learning and collaboration opportunity to take place between management and staff, which
enhances cooperation, morale, and business results.

CHECKLIST ITEM 5: MEASURE FOR DESIRED OUTCOMES

Performance measurement programs must be fine-tuned in order to work
correctly. Overdo measuring practices by attempting to measure every step
in a process, and it is like being eaten alive by a million little mosquito bites.
It is tortuous, takes too long, and may not deliver the desired outcome.
Underdo it and you would be better served to skip performance measurement altogether because it will make no difference at all.

The best approach is to conceive a performance measurement program that keeps an eye on the bigger picture and bases all measurements on desired outcomes as per the long-range vision and strategic plan, not one focused on establishing measurements for every incremental event that underpins each and every business process.

Not only does the adoption of this approach to performance measurement "right size" the program, making it easier for management and staff to use and understand but it directly supports the "tackling the whole process" concept brought out in Chapter 6, a central tenet of business transformation. Aligning performance measurement with business transformation makes sense and can bring about higher-quality changes faster than without proper alignment.

Further, driving the performance program from a desired outcomes perspective helps to define what is important to the enterprise and places emphasis on the work activities and behaviors that are most critical to overall organizational success as per its strategic vision. Sure, executives will need to set individualized expectations and ensure that every team member knows his or her job and what is anticipated from him or her; however, once that is understood, the program is easy to monitor—we are either winning the battle, or we are losing the war. See *Insurance Carrier Links Performance Measurement to Vision*, for an example from the insurance industry about the importance of tying the performance measurement program to the strategic vision of an organization.

See It in Action

Insurance Carrier Links Performance Measurement to Vision

Recently, I was working with a client that provides both business and personal insurance. Its offerings include motor vehicle and property insurance as well as life, investment, and risk management services. The company does business overseas and has over 20,000 employees.

The firm's vision calls for adding value to its customers and ensuring stakeholder satisfaction by anticipating and meeting customer needs, providing personalized products and services in the fashion and timeframe as defined by the client, and effectively managing the provision of its offerings by optimizing its own core processes.

Clearly, the responsibility for achieving these objectives does not fall solely on the shoulders of its senior executives. Rather, all staff members have a role to play. Each employee must make sure that his or her individual job is performed well and that all of his or her activities are done in ways to achieve and further the company's strategic vision.

Consequently, the firm has centered its performance measurement program on these three aspects of its vision:

✓ customer centricity
✓ product design and service delivery
✓ process optimization

To add more specificity, the insurer adopted the SMART (that is, Specific, Measureable, Achievable, Relevant, and Time-related) approach to its goal setting. SMART is a simple method of acid testing the validity of a performance goal. If a goal satisfies each of the five criteria, then it is appropriately defined and can be used as a measure of performance.

The firm defined three overarching metrics as the backbone of its performance measurement program, including:

✓ to achieve top 10 percent in customer satisfaction this year as per third-party surveys when compared with other companies in the financial services industry (customer centricity);
✓ to achieve top 20 percent of employee satisfaction this year as per third-party employee engagement surveys when compared with other companies in the financial services industry (product design and service delivery);
✓ to reduce total cost of operations by 8 percent this fiscal year (process optimization).

Focusing on these three seems to make sense. After all, customer satisfaction comes with providing the right products and services at the right time and in the right way. Happy and engaged employees will do a better job of delivering on customer satisfaction than ones that are unsatisfied and disengaged. Finding ways to reduce costs will optimize business operations and improve the bottom line.

Since each employee's individualized performance measurements roll up to one of these three SMART goals, it makes it easier for him or her to determine how best to perform the work of the enterprise. For example, if an employee finds him- or herself doing work that is not about delighting the customer, improving the work setting, or optimizing the way in which work is done, then he or she needs to ask him- or herself (and his or her management) *"Why am I doing this?"*

While it is still in its infancy, the performance measurement program does a nice job of tying vision elements to measurable results. It represents a long stride forward in aligning measurements and metrics to business strategy, helping to inform employees how best to focus their energies in the support of long-term vision achievement.

CHECKLIST ITEM 6: REWARD RESULTS

Reward and compensation programs are the other side of measurement initiatives. The two should be in lockstep to produce the best results for an organization. Since we are striving to measure against desired outcomes, as outlined above, it only makes sense to reward staff members based on their contribution to the achievement of results. Hence, compensation programs must be rethought so as to enable tracking and rewarding personnel based on results achieved, not on effort made or hours invested.

Certainly, people work hard and should be recognized when they go above and beyond in the call of duty to deliver results. However, the key words are "deliver results." If the extra effort does not provide sought-after outcomes, then what are we rewarding? My stock portfolio doesn't rise a penny in value because the staffs at the firms in which I invest are "trying hard." No, I only make money if the firms in which I invest achieve results.

The same should be true when measuring and rewarding performance within an organization—reward results, not effort.

With that said, existing reward and compensation programs may need to be reviewed and revamped so that the measurements within them are aligned with the organizational vision. Further, staff should be involved in the process to secure their buy-in and raise their awareness of the changes being adopted within the enterprise. Personnel need to understand that their reward is proportional to their contribution to delivering desired outcomes to the enterprise.

See *Jim Beam's Reward*, for an example of a compensation strategy that the company has put into place in order to link its staff members to one vision, one set of goals, and the company value of taking responsibility for business outcomes.

See It in Action

Jim Beam's Reward

Beam, Inc., headquartered in Deerfield, Illinois, crafts and markets dozens of the world's top premium spirits brands, including Jim Beam, Makers Mark, Pinnacle Vodka, and Souza Tequila, to name a few. Through acquisition, Beam has grown to become the fourth-largest premium spirits company in the world and the largest United States-based spirits company.

It is difficult to get to a "one Beam way" of doing business with a growth-through-acquisition strategy. In the words of Mindy Mackenzie, senior vice president and chief human resources officer at Beam Inc.:

"To unite the organization and improve company performance, we really needed a cultural transformation that would inspire deep employee engagement, passion and performance. We wanted to re-hydrate our culture and build a unified identity."[2]

In order to achieve that goal, Mackenzie brought in consultants to help her and her team to design and develop a reward strategy that would link all members of the Beam team to one vision, one set of goals, and, most importantly, a singular mindset of "owning" all business outcomes.

The reward system included:

✓ an employee stock purchase plan, which gave employees an easy way to become direct owners of Beam stock;
✓ performance-based bonuses;
✓ an executive incentive plan to help align all senior leaders around a common strategic plan;
✓ development of a new salary structure to further encourage collaboration, ownership, and alignment among employees

Under this compensation program, everyone gains when desired outcomes are achieved. Accordingly, management and staff now have skin in the game and are rewarded when the corporation performs well and realizes results.

The reward program at Beam, Inc. is a good illustration for all of us interested in driving change and transforming staff by aligning compensation with the long-range plans of the organization.

Source: "*Beam Inc. Reinvents Total Rewards to Support a New Global Culture,*" by Lucie P. Lawrence, Strategy at Work, towerswatson.com, November 2012.

CHECKLIST ITEM 7: REIMAGINE INCENTIVES

Clearly, bad things can happen when we don't properly compensate and incentivize our personnel. Consider recent events at Walmart, for example. Low wages and store-level downsizing have led to poor morale and, in turn, a diminished customer experience. Shoppers are leaving in multitudes, and competitors, like Costco, are enjoying growth as a consequence (For more on this, see **Wal-Mart Gets What It Pays For!**).

Indeed, incentives are an important part of inspiring the transformation of staff. Financial incentives are a natural extension of reward and compensation programs. In fact, many compensation programs have an incentive component integrated within them. However, incentives don't always need to be monetary in nature. Nonmonetary incentives can be just as effective at motivating staff and encouraging their transformation as those that provide income.

However, the identification of nonfinancial incentives does require some imagination. Here are a handful of incentive rewards that I have helped clients identify and put into practice:

- ✓ preferred parking or garage spots
- ✓ team recognition dinners
- ✓ additional personal leave time
- ✓ self-selected training classes
- ✓ tickets to sporting events
- ✓ gift cards
- ✓ company logo items
- ✓ prepaid family vacations
- ✓ self-selected conference attendance
- ✓ tickets to the Arts

These types of nonmonetary incentives can go a long way toward inspiring performance and advancing transformative change among staff members. It is up to us as executive leadership to tie these types of rewards to the organizational outcomes and workforce improvement behaviors desired.

See It in Action

Walmart Gets What It Pays For!

Walmart is the epitome of a discount retailer. Everything that it does is on the cheap. Notorious for nickel and diming suppliers, while pinching pennies with their employee compensation, Walmart is beginning to feel the impact of cutting to close to the bone.

Last year, the company grew its store count by 13 percent, while downsizing its staff by 20,000. To say that morale is suffering at the discount retailer is quite an understatement. Customer service is atrocious, while store shelves remain nearly empty as product sits on pallets waiting for stocking—prompting Walmart to rank last among department and discount stores in the American Customer Satisfaction Index.

It is no wonder that rivals like Costco are growing their sales and their membership (infact Costco increased its membership revenue by $69 million in first quarter 2013, compared to the same quarter last year). Clearly, customers are leaving Walmart in droves, seeking a better experience at Costco, where the shelves are stocked, lines are shorter, and shopper assistance is readily available.

Are poor compensation and a lack of incentive planning a trend that is contributing to the problem at Walmart? As recently as last year, Massachusetts Institute of Technology management professor Zeynep Ton reasoned in a **Harvard Business Review** article, which points to that probability, that:

"Costco and Trader Joe's pay their workers far more than many of their competitors, offer their employees opportunities for promotion and enjoy markedly lower worker turnover and far higher sales per employee than their low-road counterparts. Sales per employee at Costco are nearly double that at Sam's Club." [3]

Undeniably, personnel inform the customer experience in a retail store and Walmart's customers appear not to be very happy. Thus, maybe the discount retailer should follow Costco's lead and begin to rethink its employee compensation and incentive models in order to right the ship, while there is still a ship to right.

Source: *"Walmart Pays Workers Poorly and Sinks While Costco Pays Workers Well and Sails—Proof That You Get What You Pay For,"* by Rick Ungar, www.forbes.com, *April 17, 2013.*

CHECKLIST ITEM 8: BUILD A CREATIVE TEAM OF PERSONNEL

Thus far, our focus has been on training, measurement, and reward and their mutual interdependencies. Building a creative staff is the last element of personnel makeover. It is a fitting way to top off the three pillars of staff transformation that we've already discussed, for those pillars are further reinforced and perpetuated by fielding a creative staff.

Creativity can be knitted into the culture in a variety of ways. Sponsoring programs that promote the Arts is one approach to developing the creativity of the workforce. Exposing staff members to music, theater, and fine art can inspire change and encourage new ways of thinking and doing which, when brought to work, can improve problem-solving, enrich communications, and enhance cooperation.

Additionally, we can further help staff to cement new creative thinking into their repertoire by inspiring discussion and exploration. Subsidizing community outreach programs, hosting "lunch and learns," and promoting book clubs that focus on provocative, non-work-related topics are some principal ways to accomplish that. After all, changes in personal perceptions and attitudes are realized when we are exposed to new people and ideas. Therefore, establishing occasions for that to occur in the workplace only serves to further the cause.

Let's not forget the obvious approaches, either. Creating opportunities for working in cross-functional teams—a tactic commonly used by organizations to expand problem-solving and augment communications—can also work to advance creative thinking. This type of work setting exposes staff members to new problem-solving paradigms and thought models, which enables them to become more creative on the job.

Constructing a creative workspace within the enterprise is another obvious approach that can spark and promote creativity. On balance, our work environment directly influences our disposition and affects our ability to generate ideas and develop creative solutions. Inspiring work settings have attention-grabbing and visually stimulating elements within them. Designing such elements into the physical surroundings where work is performed can stimulate the creative juices of our staff members, too.

Unmistakably, organizations enjoy many benefits by building a more creative team of personnel, including:

✓ **Better talent**—enabled by the fashioning of a rewarding and inspiring work environment;
✓ **Better problem-solving**—brought about by the amalgam of talent that is regularly called upon to develop creative solutions to business problems;
✓ **Better product and service offerings**—facilitated by exposure to innovative ways of thinking and doing;
✓ **Better differentiation**—as a result of creative minds working together to astound.

It is important for us as executives to become passionate about forging creativity into our organizations. It certainly will not be easily accomplished (see *Creativity Sure Ain't Easy*, for some interesting findings from a recent survey on the subject). Yet by making it a priority, we can transform our staffs and establish a nourishing work environment—one that arouses and provokes exceptional performance from the entire enterprise.

See It in Action

Creativity Sure Ain't Easy

While today's ever-complex business world demands creative thinking and innovative solutions, building a creative workforce sure isn't easy. A recent survey sanctioned by Adobe Systems, Inc. reinforces the point.

Adobe's *State of Create Study* was produced by the research firm StrategyOne and conducted as an online survey among a total of 5,000 adults, 18 years or older, with 1,000 each in the United States, United Kingdom, Germany, France, and Japan. The data set for each country is nationally representative of the population of that country. Its findings show:[4]

✓ a global creativity gap exists in five of the world's largest economies;

✓ 39 percent of respondents describe themselves as creative;

✓ 75 percent believe they are not living up to their own creative potential;

✓ 75 percent of respondents say they are under growing pressure at work to be more productive and less creative;

✓ 8 in 10 people feel that unlocking creativity is critical to economic growth;

✓ lack of time is seen as the biggest barrier to creativity.

What does all of this say about the state of creativity? It would seem that, in the business setting, too much emphasis is being placed on productivity, and too little time is invested in developing the creativity needed to overcome complexities. This can be easily changed by recalibrating what we as executives deem important. For my money, nothing is more important than fostering creativity because that's where all of the breakthrough ideas that can change the world are born.

Source: *"Study Reveals Global Creativity Gap," Adobe Systems, Inc. Press Release,* www.adobe.com, *April 23, 2012.*

IN CLOSING

Staff transformation is about creating a management structure that trains, measures, and rewards personnel for delivering desired outcomes. By enabling employees to succeed and rewarding them when they do, organizations can continually expand capabilities, generate sought-after results, and nurture innovative ways of conducting the business of the enterprise.

Certainly, staff transformation efforts must be deliberate, well planned, and informed by the strategic intentions of the organization. However, creativity must be developed and instilled into the organization as well. This helps staff members to recognize more possibilities and enables them to be quicker on their feet—improving organizational agility and enhancing results.

To close, lasting success for a staff transformation program is about placing the emphasis on the "big picture" and encouraging staff to change behaviors and develop skills that are needed to make the enterprise more successful. It is a vital part of rejuvenating the current execution culture, while enabling the achievement of desired outcomes. Organizations change as people change.

RENEW COMMUNICATIONS PRACTICES—TRANSPARENCY IMPROVES PERFORMANCE

The single biggest problem in communication is the illusion that it has taken place.

—George Bernard Shaw

As referenced throughout the book, today's business environment requires that organizations learn to function at a very high level, while continuously changing and growing. The idea is to be as nimble, quick, interconnected, and customer-centric as possible, and still consistently pump out customizable products and services of unmatched quality and appeal. Sure, it is a tall order. Then again, if our enterprises can't deliver what the marketplace expects, someone else will.

Open and honest communications is a vital ingredient for success within the modern-day work setting described above. Staff members must be able to readily access all relevant information and know-how, wherever it exists, in the format desired, and have confidence in its quality in order to use it. Hence, a renewal of communications practices is not only in order but is essential to remaining competitive.

The checklist provided below outlines the essentials needed to effectively renew communications practices, enabling better organizational performance through more transparency:

> ***Communications Renewal Checklist***
>
> ✓ Know the Scope
> ✓ Promote Transparency
> ✓ Focus on the Middle Layer
> ✓ Inspire Collaboration
> ✓ Pull a Henry David Thoreau
> ✓ Harness the Informal Network
> ✓ Drive by and Open the Door
> ✓ Practice What You Preach

Let us examine how communications renewal within the enterprise can enable improved performance and enhance progress in achieving our strategic vision.

CHECKLIST ITEM 1: KNOW THE SCOPE

The scope of a communications renewal effort will vary slightly from enterprise to enterprise. However, all entities must recognize that certain communication needs are universal and should be considered to be within scope when developing a program to improve organizational communications. For instance, all comprehensive communications renewal programs must account for these communication dimensions. Consider them the "Top 10 List" of organizational communications:

1. workplace communications
2. executive communications
3. customer and stakeholder correspondence
4. personnel relations
5. public relations
6. brand management
7. reputation management
8. crisis and disaster management
9. competitive and economic intelligence
10. government reporting

Establishing a baseline that reflects where an organization is across these dimensions can help to fine-tune the actions needed to improve the communications infrastructure within a specific concern. This is best accomplished by identifying the communication devices and mechanisms in place and assessing how well each performs in providing its expected value to the organization.

Once the baseline assessment is completed, it is a matter of course to determine areas for improvement. The improvement areas identified become fodder for the communications renewal program. Each improvement item will translate into a potential project or program that can be included in the communications renewal plan.

Don't be surprised, when beginning your communications renewal baseline analysis, to discover that there is a broad variety and extensive number of communications vehicles already in place. For example, many concerns by now use email blasts, intranet portals, and social media to communicate among staff members. What may be shocking, though, is to realize that there is an overall lack of standardization and discipline when it comes to how and when these communications devices are used.

It is important to note this lack of standardization as we go about driving the communications renewal program. After all, effective communications require that information be conveyed in the form and format that is most easily exchanged and consumed among the parties involved. So, developing standards that help staff members match the message with the device is as essential to long-term results as instituting new and effective communications mechanisms (See *Pioneering CEOs Turn to Blogging*, for a sampling of one of the newer communications devices being used by some of today's major organizations).

See It in Action

Pioneering CEOs Turn to Blogging

Here are some findings from a recent survey of employees by Brandfog:[1]

✓ Seventy-seven percent believe a social CEO will increase business purchases.

✓ Seventy-eight percent want to work for a social CEO.

✓ Eighty-one percent believe that social CEOs are better leaders.

✓ Eighty-two percent believe that social CEOs are more trustworthy.

✓ Ninety-three percent believe that social CEOs are better equipped for crisis management.

✓ Ninety-four percent believe that social CEOs will enhance the company's brand.

Interesting stuff, right?

Unfortunately, it seems that many executives are a bit shy when it comes to social media and blogging in general. However, there is a growing recognition among senior executives that they need to come out of their shells a bit and embrace this new communications medium. Here are few early adopters:

✓ **Peter Aceto**—ING Direct Canada—chats about anything related to money, social media, or leadership and welcomes a dialogue with staff and clients alike in his *Direct Talk* blog found at: http://blog.ingdirect.ca/

✓ **Dan Akerson**—General Motors, GM's *FastLane* blog is a forum for GM executives to talk about GM's current and future products and services, although nonexecutives sometimes appear here to discuss the development and design of important products. On occasion, *FastLane* can be utilized to discuss other important issues facing the company. It is found at http://fastlane.gmblogs.com/

✓ **Adam Goldstein**—Royal Caribbean Cruise Lines—uses his *SeaViews* blog to discuss all aspects of cruising, giving readers an insider's perspective on cruise line management and on-board vacationing. It is found at: http://www.royalcaribbean.com/connect/blog/

✓ **Bill Marriott**—Marriott Hotels—posts useful content and commentary on topics affecting Marriott's customers and staff on his *Marriott on the Move* blog found at: http://www.blogs.marriott.com/

✓ **Bob Parsons**—GoDaddy—uses his *BobParsons.me* blog as a platform to discuss issues related to personal freedom, world issues, and Internet governance. It can be found at: http://www.bobparsons.me/index.php

✓ **Kevin Roberts**—Saatchi & Saatchi—discusses all facets of marketing, communications, and design on his *KR Connect* blog found at: http://krconnect.blogspot.com/

CEOs, like the executives outlined here, have surely gained a step on their rivals by folding social media and blogging into their communications renewal programs, leaving the rest of us to catch up.

CHECKLIST ITEM 2: PROMOTE TRANSPARENCY

It is nearly impossible to overdo communications within an enterprise. In fact, esprit de corps can be established by adopting an attitude that promotes and encourages the frequent sharing of information.

However, it is important to keep the "spin" to a minimum. Staff will not react well or trust in us as leaders if there's any sense that facts are being manipulated or that important information is being unduly withheld.

This is particularly true when it comes to communicating serious or unfavorable information to interested parties both inside and out. This type of information must be delivered as quickly as possible, or company morale and stakeholder relations will surely suffer (see *EA Is the Worst!*, for an example of what happens to firms when they don't communicate well). With all of this, it is imperative that our communications renewal program stimulates transparency while inspiring everyone to communicate regularly.

One of the ways in which we can demonstrate the desired behavior is for us as executives to be extremely inclusive in our communications. This is achieved by extending executive communications to a broader audience within the concern, including more staff in key meetings and actively soliciting input from line personnel on a consistent basis.

A platform for improved transparency can be established through increased and deliberate inclusiveness, thus enabling a means to more freely and frequently share ideas and deliver important information across the enterprise. The communications flow opens widely when management and staff members see their leaders seek, recognize, and value differences of opinion. It opens the door for employees to communicate more freely among themselves, which, in turn, enhances communications within the concern.

See It in Action

EA Is the Worst!

For the second year in a row, the consumer watchdog website The Consumerist has named Electronic Arts (EA) *"the worst company in America."* EA beat out such perennial "un-favorites" as AIG, AT&T, BP, and Halliburton for the not-so-coveted "Golden Poo" award.

While listing such common consumer gripes as:

✓ *Greedy pricing policies*—that require in-game purchasing for access to enhanced features;
✓ *Poor product quality*—due to rushing releases to market without adequate testing and completion;
✓ *Sketchy customer support*—characterized by unanswered customer complaints and questions; and
✓ *Unmet consumer demands*—as exemplified by the unwarranted promotion and release of game sequels that few people want to play

as reasons that contributed to the "win," perhaps the greatest reason for customer revolt is related to the dismissive and haughty communications of its executive team.

To quote the site:[2]

"Perhaps EA is secretly of the school of thought that there is no such thing as bad publicity. That's the only way to explain the decision by Peter Moore, the company's chief operating officer, to release one of the most defensive, deflective, non-apology apologies we've ever seen."

Whether the message received by EA's consumer base is what was intended by Moore when he responded to recent complaints about the company is not the point. Rather, what is relevant is that his response managed to aggravate EA's devotees and infuriate the industry pundits who "spin" the "spin" for their clientele.

Our takeaway from this is to be as thoughtful and as transparent as possible with our communications, because any sign of defensiveness or excuse-making during difficult times only serves to incense and raise suspicions among our stakeholders. While the truth sometimes hurts, skirting issues and laying blame is not good for business either. Open and honest is the way to go!

Source: *EA Makes Worst Company in American History, Wins Title for Second Year in a Row!*, by Chris Morran, www.consumerist.com, *April 9, 2013.*

CHECKLIST ITEM 3: FOCUS ON THE MIDDLE LAYER

There are three management layers in many organizations. The executive layer sits at the top of the pyramid and is responsible for setting direction and envisioning what the enterprise can be in the future. The midlevel managers sit in the middle layer of the organization and are most concerned about translating what is envisioned by the executives into actions that will lead to operational excellence each year. Supervisory management make up the lower layer of the management structure and are responsible for day-to-day execution. It is their work that ultimately delivers value to the customer.

The communications renewal battle is won and lost at the middle layer of the organization. Mid-tier managers either encourage open and honest communications or they work to close it down in order to maintain control and dominance over the people whom they are responsible for managing. Information sharing is squelched in work environments in which midlevel managers exhibit restricted communication behavior.

Therefore, we need to take aim at the middle. After all, staff members model the behaviors of their leaders. If the leader seeks out opinions and solicits input, then personnel will naturally cooperate with each other, too; if the leader hides and hordes information, then personnel will follow suit for fear of reprisal.

To extend the point, it is common to find that communications, teamwork, and cooperation are exceptional within a specific department. However, cross-department communication and teaming is often strained or nonexistent. This is a common characteristic in many places. It is often a symptom of organizational silos (as described in Chapter 6). In such work settings, information is hidden away and kept secret from other departments for a multitude of parochial motives.

We need to focus attention on helping the middle layer understand why communications is vital to the organization's continuing success and convince them that better information sharing across the enterprise will lead to a higher degree of cooperation. Increased cooperation will make their jobs more enjoyable and easier to perform. *Trouble on High at JCPenney* highlights what happens when executives fail to engage the middle layers of an organization.

See It in Action

Trouble on High at JCPenney

JCPenney may have been slipping, but it was stable when Ron Johnson took the helm as its CEO in November 2011. Sensing complacency within the workforce, he wanted to transform the retailer. So, he and his management team developed a vision that called for a total transformation of the department store giant, one that would attract a younger, hipper crowd.

That all sounds good. But Johnson and his team did not communicate the needed changes very well to JCPenney's middle managers. Consequently, rumors of sweeping change engulfed the firm. Personnel, from store managers on down to sales associates working on the floor, began to panic.

Here are some quotes from anonymous staff members that illustrate the situation[3]:

✓ *"There is no protocol or process in the company anymore."*
✓ *"The direction given on product changes very frequently."*

✓ *"They do not leave any opportunity for anyone to ask questions."*

✓ *"While working at the home office, we do not get any insight to store operations and changes."*

✓ *"There are no memos or written directives anymore."*

✓ *"Everything gets communicated verbally and without too much detail."*

All of this dread and concern translated into dismal performance at the retailer. Workers became spooked, service diminished, and customers left in droves. Therefore, it is no surprise that the stock price went down an eye-popping 46 percent from 2012. By all accounts, Johnson's ill-communicated vision for the future and his transformation strategies failed.

No one knows for sure, why Johnson and his team failed so miserably to engage the middle management layer of the Company. But it is no wonder that on April 8, 2013, Myron E. (Mike) Ullman, III, the department store's previous chief executive was rehired, out of retirement, and named CEO at JCPenney.

Johnson's story helps to emphasize the importance of focusing communications on the middle management of the enterprise.

Source: *"INSIDE JCPENNEY: Widespread Fear, Anxiety, and Distrust of Ron Johnson and His New Management Team,"* by *Kim Bhasin, Business Insider, February 22, 2013.*

CHECKLIST ITEM 4: INSPIRE COLLABORATION

The responsibility for setting a collaborative tone starts at the top. Largely, an organization's vision story (as described in Chapter 3) stresses teamwork and cooperation and describes a work setting rich in collaboration. The communications renewal program should parlay that focus and design communication elements into the organizational culture that inspire and enable collaboration across the enterprise.

There are technology-driven communications solutions available that integrate mobile, social, and graphical features of collaboration.

This allows personnel to come together anytime from anywhere, independent of platform. An insurance company, for example, can conduct a meeting with some colleagues in a video conference center in Warren, New Jersey, one on an iPad in Bangalore, and with three people on smartphones logged into a hotspot in Amsterdam. They can all see each other, share information through a virtual whiteboard, and interact as if they were all in the same room. This type of collaborative communication strategy has a far-reaching impact. Some of the byproducts provided through a communication environment that inspires collaboration, include:

✓ increased communication throughout the enterprise;
✓ enhanced workforce relations and productivity;
✓ stronger trust and understanding among cross-functional teams;
✓ accelerated and better quality decision-making;
✓ gains in organizational knowledge through membership in interactive communities;
✓ improved customer interactions and responsiveness.

Companies like Philips Electronics provide wonderful examples of how businesses can institute collaborative communication strategies through the implementation of the right technology. See *Philips Does Collaboration Right!*, for a current example.

See It in Action

Philips Does Collaboration Right!

Royal Philips Electronics employs 116,000 people in more than 60 countries. It provides a world-class portfolio of healthcare, lifestyle, and lighting products. A few years ago, it decided to embrace collaboration technology that would allow Philips' executive committee in the Netherlands to stay in close contact with managers elsewhere around the globe.

In the words of Jap Jongedijk, Deputy Secretary, Philips Executive Committee[4]:

"Our vision was a state-of-the-art multifunctional boardroom, combining everything we needed to integrate video conferencing and multimedia into our management meeting cycle."

It chose Cisco Telepresence to do the job.

Cisco Telepresence is a high-definition (HD) video-conferencing experience that delivers realistic virtual meetings. It creates the illusion that participants are in the same room, when in fact they may be in different cities or on different continents. Telepresence delivers high-impact, realistic meetings with similar room setups at each site (including furniture and décor), HD video and audio, and large display devices. In most cases, a Telepresence installation is an easily deployed solution that is integrated into a dedicated room.

The benefits of embracing the technology were immediately obvious:

✓ *Better Use of Time*—Less time is spent traveling and more time is spent problem-solving.

✓ *Lower Travel Expenses*—It costs less to stage a meeting using Telepresence than it does to move people around the globe in order to meet in person.

✓ *Faster Decision-Making*—The technology enables organizations to bring experts together to solve problems on the fly. The sooner people can begin working out solutions, the faster they reach decisions.

✓ *More Collaboration*—Telepresence offers the easiest way for dispersed teams to work together to get things done.

The executive committee now functions even more effectively as the hub of a global wheel of virtual communications, enabling better all-round business coordination. Royal Philips Electronics is well equipped to make top-level use of instant collaborative communications, allowing it to stay on top in a rough-and-tumble business environment.

Source: *Philips Advocates Board-Level Global Collaboration,* by Cisco Systems, Inc., http://www.cisco.com/en/US/prod/collateral/ps7060/ps8329/ps9573 /royal_philips_electronics.pdf, *September 7, 2012.*

CHECKLIST ITEM 5: PULL A HENRY DAVID THOREAU

In his seminal work **Walden**, Henry David Thoreau told us all to: *"Simplify! Simplify! Simplify!"* It is certainly sound advice, at least in how it relates to communications renewal. Who are we to argue with this great American author, poet, and philosopher anyway?

We need to keep our communication strategies and apparatus simple. The simpler we make it to communicate, the more communication will be invoked and the higher degree of organizational effectiveness will be achieved. As has been already mentioned, we must promote regular, open, and honest communications by making use of the right devices, in the right way at the right time.

We must enable the free flow of information by establishing an easy-to-use and understand communications infrastructure that has the following capabilities designed into its very foundation:

✓ **push facility**—the ability to deliver information to those who need to know without any direct involvement necessary by the recipient, essential for getting critical information out to concerned parties

✓ **pull facility**—the ability for staff to request information and "pull" it through the delivery channel as they desire, which is critical to the management of communications flow

✓ **instantaneous conveyance**—the ability to communicate instantly, which is needed when immediate response is required

✓ **multidirectional**—the ability to broadcast and receive communications to and from a wide variety of stakeholders, which is central to managing most business operations

✓ **multichannel**—the ability to use multiple distribution channels to convey communications, which is indispensable in today's highly interconnected business world

With so much information flying at us from all corners of the globe, it is easy to become overwhelmed. Therefore, designing a communications framework and supporting substructure that can both promote proper communications and manage potential information overload is imperative.

A design that possesses the characteristics outlined above can go a long way toward simplifying what are otherwise considered sophisticated communication approaches. Take a look at *Wipro Retail Keeps It Simple* for a present-day illustration of the possibilities available for keeping it simple.

See It in Action

Wipro Retail Keeps It Simple!

Wipro Ltd. is a global information technology, consulting, and outsourcing company with 140,000 employees serving over 900 clients in 57 countries. The company posted revenues of $7.37 billion for the financial year ended March 31, 2012. Wipro Retail is a division of Wipro Technologies. Its staff members provide information technology and business services to the retail sector.

Analysis within the division showed that employees were receiving far too many internal emails. This was affecting employee productivity. More significantly, important internal messages were often overlooked. Consequently, the division had to find a solution to reduce internal email volumes and still ensure that important messages reached and were being read by its personnel.

So, it looked to the New Zealand-based SnapComms' SnapMag tool for relief. SnapMag permits internal messages, intended for more than a few recipients, to be easily aggregated into a 'one-stop' staff magazine format, allowing for fewer interrupts per week and enabling staff members to scroll and scan the aggregated messages for topics of specific interest to them.

In addition to reducing internal email volumes, SnapMag offers other benefits as well:

✓ Each SnapMag article / message can have a unique expiry time and be automatically removed from the staff magazine (and employee computers) after a defined period of time. This helps to reduce message volume, data storage, and archiving times.
✓ Staff can search a database and revisit past articles.

✓ Articles are "user generated"; hence the time and resources to produce an internal staff magazine can be dramatically reduced.

✓ Employee involvement can help break down silos and improve communications across the concern.

✓ New editions of a magazine can bypass email altogether and be promoted as scrolling desktop news feeds to ensure message delivery.

✓ Reporting on which articles are being read, and by whom, helps to optimize the channel.

Wipro Retail's use of the SnapComm technology paints a vivid picture of how organizations can communicate widely, yet keep it simple and effective. All of us can learn to do the same in our communications renewal efforts.

Source: *Innovative Digital Tools Help Wipro Retail Conquer Internal Email Overload,* by SnapComms, http://www.snapcomms.com/case-studies/internal-email-overload-case-study.pdf, *April 13, 2011.*

CHECKLIST ITEM 6: HARNESS THE INFORMAL NETWORK

The informal communications network, or in-house grapevine, is an inevitable part of every organization. Without a doubt, it is difficult to control and nearly impossible to measure and monitor. Information is regularly diffused throughout an entity by word of mouth. So, we can't expect to stop the flow of communications through informal means. We have to learn how to harness its power—and remind ourselves that it is not all bad.

After all, the grapevine sustains personal relationships among staff members and can be a powerful tool for taking the pulse of the enterprise and disseminating information. The personal interactions that take place though the informal communications network strengthen working relationships, build trust, and can resolve subtleties in communication among staff members.

Sure, the in-house grapevine can be unscrupulous at times because of the rumor and gossip that is peddled through it. However, we can take steps to minimize rumor and gossip—two things that will negatively impact morale and productivity—by doing a better job of ensuring that formal communication are less ambiguous and more to the point.

Rumors begin where there is a lack of information and detail. It is human nature to fill in gaps in knowledge with assumptions, suppositions, and inferences, all of which are provender for rumors and gossip. Hence, if we improve the quality and effectiveness of formal communications, our informal communications will improve as well.

With rumors and gossip neutralized, the best way to harness the grapevine is to jump right on board. Unquestionably, there is a communication gap between superiors and their subordinates. But the gap can be closed through superiors' having more frequent face-to-face communication, speaking a common language, and becoming part of the grapevine.

If we choose to introduce technology that enables easier information exchanges across the informal communications structure, then more people can join in the conversation. This, in turn, provides a way for us as executives to establish more interpersonal relationships within the enterprise, as well. As an added bonus, it also increases our credibility along the way.

CHECKLIST ITEM 7: DRIVE BY AND OPEN THE DOOR

Continuing on the theme above, doing "drive-bys" is another way for us as executives to leverage informal communications while promoting honest and candid information sharing across our organizations. Why limit our communications time to regularly scheduled meetings or standard correspondence when we can regularly gauge the pulse of the enterprise by walking around and engaging our people in conversations about the work that they do and the understanding that they have of the organization's goals and objectives?

Further, it is fine to drop in on project teams while in workshop and during project meetings. It is a "morale booster" when staff members come to realize that their senior leaders are personally interested in the work that they do. This type of "management by walking around" also provides an opportunity for personnel to discuss their contributions that they are making to the cause. It goes a long way toward enhancing communications within the concern.

Along with the "drive-bys," executives are advised to maintain an open-door policy to the greatest extent possible. By keeping the door wide open, we demonstrate approachability (a trait we want our middle- and lower-level managers to exhibit as well) and promote transparency. We can establish a winning atmosphere by giving them the time they need to express opinions and discuss issues that they deem important and essential.

After all, communications is a two-way street. It is only effective when the parties involved mutually understand the meaning intended. Executives must work assiduously to establish the communication environment that they want within their organizations. Coupling "drive-bys" with an open-door policy goes a long way toward substantiating commitment to direct and transparent communications.

CHECKLIST ITEM 8: PRACTICE WHAT YOU PREACH

Despite our best intentions, though, "drive-bys" and open-door policies may not be enough. Therefore, it is essential that we go out of our way to practice what we preach. This means that we, too, must communicate with our staffs and use the tools and protocols that are in place in the most effective ways possible. As mentioned, subordinates model the behaviors of their superiors. Thus, it is our obligation to lead the way in regard to establishing solid communications within our organizations. For example, here are a handful of ideas that can be used to communicate the enterprise's vision and strategies:

✓ **Video Links**—This technique is gaining popularity as more and more organizations are creating videos and distributing all kinds of content via websites and portals. A video link published on a company's intranet site can be an effective way of distributing the vision briefing. However, the practice may be less effective in organizations that have workers who don't directly use computers in their jobs. Therefore, additional communications methods may be required to augment the video blog technique of vision socialization.

It can be part of a suite of communication devices used to keep everyone informed.

✓ **Town Hall Meetings**—This approach gathers all staff together and briefs them on the vision and company progress. It's a solid way of reinforcing the vision and reminding staff members how they fit in. Superiors can describe in some detail the types of changes needed to achieve the vision.

Larger organizations with thousands of employees spread across multiple geographical locations may choose to simulcast town hall meetings, or schedule several town hall meetings and conduct them locally over the course of a few weeks. Regardless, it's important that staff members be given a chance to hear information directly from a leader and not secondhand.

✓ **Employee Communication Push Channels**—Tools like Corporate Screensaver Messaging, Desktop Alerts, and Desktop Tickers can be very effective and easy-to-use "push" tools for distributing vision and strategy information throughout the organization. Used correctly, these employee communication channels serve to engage and enlighten staff, while ensuring that every employee receives the same information at the same time.

✓ **Lunch and Learns**—Staff are invited to these lunchtime information sessions and asked to bring a lunch to eat while they participate in a meeting with the leader. This is a low-key way of encouraging people within the concern to understand what the vision is about and the role that they can play in helping to achieve it. While this technique is more effective in smaller groups, because it provides a more intimate setting that promotes discussion, a series of "Lunch and Learns" can be scheduled and conducted over a period of time to ensure everyone has been able to participate in one of the sessions.

✓ **Executive Blogs**—As discussed earlier, this communications device is rising in popularity among senior leaders. Published regularly, either on an enterprise's intranet or Internet site, it is a superb way for executives to provide perspective on an organization's current strategic efforts. Because the writing style for most blogs is casual and less structured than archetypal business correspondence, blogs also offer a means to help personnel to see their senior leaders in another light, one that is more relaxed and apt to reinforce an executive's commitment to communication transparency.

✓ **Social Media**—Executive communications can be distributed using social media outlets to great effect. Social media channels like Twitter, Facebook, and LinkedIn are all fine ways to publish executive-generated content. Unlike blogging, they provide a platform for interaction. When used to discuss vision and strategy, internal social media tools like SharePoint provide an opportunity for staff to correspond and debate with their leadership in a less threatening setting than can be provided through in-person interaction.

✓ **Disciple Model**– A leader must create a formal way in which to drive important information into the enterprise from the top down. This begins with the leader providing key messaging to his or her senior subordinates and charging each subordinate to brief his or her direct reports on its content. They, in turn, do the same until every employee has been briefed by his or her manager. It's a terrific way to communicate important information and engage each management layer of an enterprise in the process. For more on the Disciple Model, see *Getting the Word Out at The Hartford*.

Using these types of communication devices offers ways to practice what we preach. That said, it is important that we match the message to the right communications device. Sharing our corporate strategy via Facebook is probably ill-advised. However, starting a conversation for soliciting bright ideas for process improvements can be done via the company's intranet site in a very effective way.

See It in Action

Getting the Word Out at The Hartford

A few years ago, I worked with The Hartford on recasting its Property & Casualty claims operation. The management team had developed a new vision that called for the breakdown of unit-level silos and increased teaming. It changed how the 3,000 staff members were organized and how they were to perform their duties.

While commonsensical from an outsider's perspective, the prescribed changes were considered radical by many in the company. Therefore, it was imperative that we get the word out in the most effective way possible. Because the staff were spread out across the country and worked out of over 80 field offices, vision socialization was going to be a challenge. A "Disciple Model" was selected to be used as a way to personalize the message to the troops.

A solid briefing outlining the vision and describing the new way work would be done was drafted and delivered to the department's senior management team. Each senior manager was asked to become very familiar with the presentation materials and deliver the briefing to his or her direct reports at the next scheduled staff meetings. Once accomplished, the next management tier was directed to do the same and deliver the vision briefing to their teams.

The vision was driven down into the department in this way— managers briefing supervisors, supervisors briefing staff members— until everyone within the department was informed on where it was going and how each person fit into the vision.

The Disciple Model proved to be an effective method of communicating the vision to each staff member in an organized, but comfortable, way—one that served to engage and involve, rather than intimidate and threaten. It is a wonderful example of how transparent communications can be accomplished across a large and geographically dispersed work environment.

TO CLOSE

As discussed throughout the chapter, inadequate communication systems result in miscommunication and missed opportunities; however, creating a work setting that willingly shares information and is transparent improves staff motivation and leads to better performance. Thus, we must make a concerted effort to renew our communication programs and institute the appropriate mechanisms and devices to make the sharing of information more natural and easier to accomplish.

Initially, middle managers may need to be pressured to play along. To reiterate, they make or break communication strategy within any enterprise. Their reluctance to share information for fear of losing influence and control must be overcome. However, when they are on board, there is no stopping an organization's information flow. In fact, there will likely be a need to seek out newer technological approaches just to keep up.

Once these newer devices are in place, no one, not even the executive team, should be above using them to communicate the right information in the right ways to all who have a need to know. After all, this is how we break down the barriers of communication and enable collaboration.

In the end, communication is a competence that every organization must develop in order to stay sharp, remain focused, and be better positioned to readily seize marketplace opportunities as they arise. A communications renewal program that embraces the ideas and theories outlined above not only improves communications competence but also enables a more open work environment to emerge, one that values the active participation of its employees and increases their sense of being in it together.

It all adds up to a winning combination that is tough to beat!

REIMAGINE THE ORGANIZATION— THE EXPRESSWAY TO THE FUTURE

Imagination is everything. It is the preview of life's coming attractions.
—Albert Einstein

Most of today's organizational designs are a derivative of the "command-and-control" reporting structure that was borrowed from the military by industry over a century ago. The model prevails to this day because it clearly delineates *"who's the boss."* While its strict definition of reporting lines and demarcation of decision-making responsibility provides clarity to the enterprise, it also serves to limit an organization's strategic dexterity and speed of change.

Therefore, it just may be time to reimagine the organization and deem the command and control organizational model, and all of its offshoots, obsolete. A shift to more cooperative-based models makes better sense because they provide greater autonomy and freedom of choice in the way work is managed and executed—a characteristic that needs to be woven into the fabric of every organization that wants greater marketplace agility and all of the benefits that come with an empowered workforce.

Here is a checklist that can be used to reimagine today's organizations:

Organization Reimagination Checklist
✓ Rethink the Pyramid Structure.
✓ Consider Team-based and Networked Organizational Designs.

✓ Head toward Freelancer-rich Operating Models.

✓ Recognize the Challenges of Alternative Designs.

✓ Recruit to the Strategic Vision.

✓ Attract and Incentivize with Training.

✓ Retain through Innovative Work-setting Changes.

✓ Reexamine the Vendor Connection.

Let's begin our consideration of why reimagining organizational design is a necessary step toward forging the expressway to the future.

CHECKLIST ITEM 1: RETHINK THE PYRAMID STRUCTURE

A multilayered pyramid structure is the predominant organizational design of today. It is popular because it facilitates and supports the use of command-and-control management approaches. However, the pyramid is becoming increasingly inefficient because it characteristically builds layers of management within it. Decision-making and quick response are made difficult when we have an organizational structure that reinforces the bureaucracy through its "managers managing managers" design.

It is clear that the pyramid organizational design needs to be rethought and gradually replaced with a more fluid and responsive management model—one that can withstand the stresses of the modern-day business world and still adequately respond to marketplace demands in ways that keep the enterprise competitive and vital. Flatter, modular, and more cooperative-based organizational designs will need to be forged to satisfactorily replace the pyramid.

It is foolhardy to think that the shift will be accomplished overnight. After all, it has taken decades upon decades to build some of the huge, multinational organizational empires that are in place today. It will take ample time and careful planning to supplant these structures and install new, more innovative organizational designs.

Indeed, these kinds of changes transpire one step at a time. There are strong signs that the shift is beginning, even among the largest of concerns. Executives from all over the world are recognizing that organizational design changes are needed in order for their organizations to remain competitive. It is time for all of us to accept the inevitable and focus our collective attentions on beginning this aspect of organizational transformation. See *GE Aviation Shifts to a Flatter Organizational Design*, for an example of what a large conglomerate like General Electric is doing to flatten the pyramid in one of its larger divisions.

See It in Action

GE Aviation Shifts to a Flatter Organizational Design

General Electric's GE Aviation is headquartered in Cincinnati, Ohio. It is a leading producer of commercial and military jet engines and components, as well as integrated digital, electric power, and mechanical systems for aircraft. GE Aviation also has a global service network to support these offerings. Working out of over 80 locations worldwide, its 39,000 employees helped the firm generate over $17 billion in revenue in 2010.

According to a recent Wall Street Journal Online article, the manufacturer is flattening its organizational design[1]:

"For years General Electric Company has run some aviation-manufacturing facilities with no foremen or shop-floor bosses. The industrial giant says it uses the system to boost productivity in low-volume factories with a relatively small number of employees, each of whom can do several tasks.

One leader, the plant manager, sets production goals and helps resolve problems but doesn't dictate daily workflow. Teams, whose members volunteer to take on various duties, meet before and after each shift to discuss the work to be done and address problems to be solved… The team structure is being expanded to all of GE Aviation's 83 supply-chain sites, which employ 26,000."

The move can be considered exceptionally gutsy when you contemplate how fierce the competition is in jet engine manufacturing. Rivals like Rolls-Royce and Pratt & Whitney are eager to gobble up market share whenever they can. A slip-up of any magnitude could bring GE Aviation to its knees. The executive team's willingness to shift to a flatter organizational design is testament to the fact that they recognize that even the largest of enterprises must make structural, reporting-line changes in order to remain competitive.

When should we make the move?

Source: "*Who's the Boss? There Isn't One,*" by Rachel Emma Silverman, The Wall Street Journal Online, http://online.wsj.com/home-page, June 19, 2012.

CHECKLIST ITEM 2: CONSIDER TEAM-BASED AND NETWORKED ORGANIZATIONAL DESIGNS

As mentioned above, some variations of team-based organizational designs are beginning to take shape in industry. They allow for temporary worker groupings, with flatter reporting structures to be used in place of the pyramid. Team-based models can be networked and modularized so as to be more fluid and responsive than other organizational design approaches.

In fact, team-based organizational designs can be considered the next evolutionary step in business structure, surpassing even the "matrixed" organization that has gained prominence in recent years. A matrixed organization calls for the employee pool to concurrently report to, and work with, multiple managers based on workload and business priorities. While flatter than the pyramid, it is the management of competing priorities that lends to confusion, inconsistencies, and slow response in matrixed structures.

On the other hand, a team-based, networked structure organizes work into projects. For example, projects are grouped into portfolios. A team is assigned to each portfolio. Each team forms a node in the network. Key knowledge workers can be permanently assigned to a node, facilitating deep-rooted understanding of a portfolio's particular focus, while subject matter experts are moved in and out of nodes on a just-in-time basis, providing a means for the enterprise to better leverage specialized expertise across all of its work.

Resembling a hub and spoke when mapped out on paper, with the hub being the executive and administrative layer and each spoke being a node led by supervisors charged with driving the projects within the assigned portfolio, a team-based, networked structure provides for quicker decision-making and increased scalability when compared to other organizational design alternatives. Take a look at *W. L. Gore & Associates Innovative Organizational Design*, for an example of a networked design in action.

See It in Action

W. L. Gore & Associates Innovative Organizational Design

Known for its Gore-Tex product line, W. L. Gore & Associates, Inc. was founded on January 1, 1958, in Newark, Delaware, by Bill and Genevieve Gore. It is a privately held company that has a presence throughout the world. Gore employs more than 10,000 associates, with manufacturing facilities in the United States, Germany, the United Kingdom, Japan, and China, and with sales offices around the world. Its combined sales in the past fiscal year exceeded $3 billion.

In 2012, Gore earned the number eight spot on the World's Best Multinational Workplaces list by the Great Place to Work® Institute. The ranking is the world's largest annual study of workplace excellence and identifies the top 25 best multinational companies in terms of workplace culture.

Interestingly, W.L. Gore & Associates is organized as a team-based network. Here is how the company describes its culture and organizational design on its website:[2]

"How we work at Gore sets us apart. Since Bill Gore founded the company in 1958, Gore has been a team-based, flat lattice organization that fosters personal initiative. There are no traditional organizational charts, no chains of command, nor predetermined channels of communication.

Instead, we communicate directly with each other and are accountable to fellow members of our multi-disciplined teams. We encourage hands-on innovation, involving those closest to a project in decision making. Teams organize around opportunities and leaders emerge. This unique kind of corporate structure has proven to be a significant contributor to associate satisfaction and retention.

We work hard at maximizing individual potential, maintaining an emphasis on product integrity, and cultivating an environment where creativity can flourish. A fundamental belief in our people and their abilities continues to be the key to our success.

How does all this happen? Associates (not employees) are hired for general work areas. With the guidance of their sponsors (not bosses) and a growing understanding of opportunities and team objectives, associates commit to projects that match their skills. All of this takes place in an environment that combines freedom with cooperation and autonomy with synergy.

Everyone can earn the credibility to define and drive projects. Sponsors help associates chart a course in the organization that will offer personal fulfillment while maximizing their contribution to the enterprise. Leaders may be appointed, but are defined by 'followership.' More often, leaders emerge naturally by demonstrating special knowledge, skill, or experience that advances a business objective."

Gore's organizational design is almost as innovative as the products that the firm is known for. The fact that it is regularly recognized as a great place to work demonstrates that a networked design not only helps firms remain successful but also contributes to staff member job satisfaction. Perhaps, it is the interconnection of organizational design and a satisfied workforce that is the company's secret to continued growth and prosperity?

Certainly, the possibility is something for all of us to consider.

Source: "A Team-Based, Flat Lattice Organization" by W. L. Gore & Associates, as presented at http://www.gore.com/en_xx/aboutus/culture/ on May 13, 2013.

CHECKLIST ITEM 3: HEAD TOWARD FREE-LANCER-RICH OPERATING MODELS

It is important to note the distinction between an organizational design and its associated operating model. The organizational design defines how workers are grouped together, structured, and managed. The operating model defines how the organizational design is traversed in order to perform the work of the enterprise. In other words, the operating model outlines how the organization operates.

Thus, organizational design changes can call for new kinds of operating models. Similarly, societal changes can impact an organization's operating model, too. For example, recent economic downturns, coupled with the emergence of the Generation Y worker, as discussed in Chapter 4, have established a more transient workforce than existed in the most recent past. Therefore, operating models must shift to accommodate this phenomenon.

Part-time and temporary work programs are making freelance workers more the norm than ever before. Because Millennials are willing to trade the apparent security of traditional work arrangements for the independence that comes with free agency, executive leaders should anticipate the continuation and growth of the free agent workforce and, therefore, need to head toward the creation of freelancer-rich operating models. For more evidence that this trend is likely to continue, please review the ***Findings from Kelly Services' Talent Project***.

Fortunately, this type of operating model complements the team-based, network design discussed above, very well. However, there are some considerations to manage when using an operating model that regularly swaps talent in and out of the enterprise as business needs dictate, including:

✓ the need to raise awareness among permanent staff of the trends taking shape in the employment marketplace, and the organization's desire to leverage the opportunities that exist there;

✓ the need to establish assimilation programs that create a culture that attracts high-quality free agent personnel and gets them up to speed quickly and effectively;

✓ the need to review and reengineer business processes in order to allow work to be done remotely;

✓ the need to adjust work management and performance monitoring to accommodate remote freelancers;

✓ the executive team's promotion of this cultural shift and proactive management of the enterprise through this evolutionary step toward the freelancer-rich operating model.

Developing and implementing solutions for addressing these operating model considerations will strengthen the organizational design transformation as well. The more we can anticipate and address questions and concerns before they arise, the smoother the transition will be and the more confident our workforce will become in our decision to change the way work is managed and performed.

See It in Action

Findings from Kelly Services' Talent Project

Kelly Services, Inc. is a leader in providing workforce solutions. It offers a comprehensive array of outsourcing and consulting services, as well as world-class staffing on a temporary, temporary-to-hire, and direct-hire basis. Its 7,000-plus workforce serves clients around the globe, providing employment to more than 560,000 employees annually. The firm's 2012 revenue was in excess of $5.5 billion, so it is doing some things extremely well.

One of the things that it does very well is centralize its best thinking, and that of its strategic partners, in one place, called the Talent Project. With content available online and accessible via a smartphone app, it is a terrific resource for gaining ideas and perspective on many workplace challenges. Here are some interesting free agent workforce findings published recently by Kelly Services through its Talent Project:[3]

✓ Forty-four percent of the currently active US workforce are free agents;

✓ Forty-five percent of currently active free agents are independent contractors;

✓ Twenty-three percent of currently active free agents are sole proprietors with no staff;

✓ Twenty-one percent of currently active free agents are temporary employees;

✓ Thirty-five percent of currently active free agents possess a master's degree or higher;

✓ Seventy-seven percent of currently active free agents possess a professional or technical skill set;

✓ Seventy-three percent of currently active free agents chose free agency for its lifestyle benefits;

✓ The number of free agents in the United States has increased by seventy percent since 2008;

If these statistics are even broadly close to accurate, then there is no question about the need to forge new, freelancer-rich operating models within our organizations. The only real question that these findings suggest is, *"How quickly can we institute the necessary changes to accommodate this emerging labor force so it can be leveraged for competitive gain?"*

Source: *"The New Workforce: Insights into the Free Agent Work Style"* by the Talent Project, http://www.slideshare.net/thetalentproject/the-free-agent-workforce, September 21, 2011.

CHECKLIST ITEM 4: RECOGNIZE THE CHALLENGES OF ALTERNATIVE DESIGNS

With all that the flatter, team-based organizational structures have going for them and with their implementation being further encouraged by operating model changes spurred on by a developing free agent workforce trend, it is essential to recognize that networked designs come with their challenges, too. Here are some of the potential disadvantages and limitations of flatter designs that must be addressed when contemplating your enterprise's safe passage to an alternative organizational structure:

✓ **Increased vulnerability to execution failure**: Flatter reporting structures bring with them broader spans of control and less direct personnel oversight, so performance can suffer if safeguards aren't designed into the way work is done within each node.

✓ **Reduced workflow management**: If centralized work coordination measures aren't put in place as a shared service for use by all networked teams, then cross-enterprise workflow management can be put at risk, as there are fewer management layers available to monitor and manage workflow in flatter organizations.

✓ **Greater communication and morale challenges**: There can be less intimacy among leadership and staff, as the organizational structure is spread wider unless steps are taken to develop more effective communication devices (see Chapter 9 for some ideas about what can be done) and to better prepare staff members to accept the empowerment that comes in a team-based organizational model.

✓ **Lessened productivity**: If teams become too large to manage properly, productivity will suffer unless team members determine ways to drive and track desired performance among themselves (see *Boss-free at Valve Corporation*, for an example of how manager-less teams can effectively function in industry).

✓ **Poorer quality**: Without a doubt, quality can suffer if work processes are too complex to manage in a networked fashion, so we need to be sure that work processes are optimized before we establish new ways of being organized.

Clearly, recognizing the inherent challenges of alternative organizational designs is as important as understanding the designs themselves. We can surely head off any limits that are innate to those structures by proactively identifying them and developing solutions to preempt those weaknesses from affecting our organizational effectiveness.

See It in Action

Boss-free at Valve Corporation

Valve Corporation of Bellevue, Washington, is an entertainment software and technology company founded in 1996. In addition to creating several of the world's most award-winning games, its 300 staff members have developed leading-edge technologies, including the Source game engine and Steam, a premier online gaming platform.

Here's how Valve describes its work environment on its website:[4]

"We've been boss-free since 1996—Imagine working with super smart, super talented colleagues in a free-wheeling, innovative environment—no bosses, no middle management, no bureaucracy...Just highly motivated peers coming together to make cool stuff. It's amazing what creative people can come up with when there's nobody there telling them what to do."

What makes the firm even more interesting is the way in which it carries out its mission. Outfitting personnel with desks-on-wheels collaboration and free-form teaming are encouraged. But the firm's unique idiosyncrasies go even further. To quote a recent piece about the company that appeared in The Huffington Post:[5]

"Pay is based on employees ranking each other—but not themselves— as far as who creates the most value for the company. The entire team also participates in decisions of who to hire or fire...with its system of codependency and equality proving rather profitable: Its employee manual says profitability is 'higher than that of Google or Amazon or Microsoft.'"

If all of this sounds a bit *"New Age-y,"* perchance it is. However, the firm continues to crank out software that people respond to and want. So, it is conceivable that Valve is onto something truly revolutionary and transformational in its approach to organizational design and team management.

Sources: *"We've been boss-free since 1996," by Valve Corporation, as presented at* http://www.valvesoftware.com/company/people.html *on May 13, 2013.*

"Valve Corp., The Boss-Less Company Where Employees Run the Ship," by Drew Guarini, The Huffington Post, June 20, 2012.

CHECKLIST ITEM 5: RECRUIT TO THE STRATEGIC VISION

Given today's competitive realities, executives are hard-pressed to think more broadly about the skills, competences, and capabilities required to achieve their organization's strategic vision and forge the right structural design. For instance, the skills and capabilities needed to grow and thrive tomorrow are likely to be much different than the ones needed to maintain the status quo of today.

Subsequently, adopting an approach to hire just to meet today's needs can be tantamount to staffing for failure, while recruiting to the strategic vision can be viewed as a form of investment in the future health and prosperity of the enterprise. So, when reimagining the organization, it is best to recruit to the strategic vision. This facilitates a more supple approach to pattern and contour future organizational designs and corporate culture, as well.

Yes, as mentioned above, the full complement of talent required to remain successful for years to come will be gained through the proper blending of in-house and free agent talent. However, striking the right balance between the two is where we as executives need to creatively lead. The better we manage that balance, the better our organizations become over time.

Determining which skills, competences, and capabilities to invest in and grow in-house from the ones that can be acquired, as needed, from outside can be a challenge. However, using the strategic vision as a guide will not only help to inform those choices, but it can be used as a means to attract and hire staff in a more purposeful and deliberate way.

With the latest advancements in technology and social media, there are limitless ways in which firms enlist talent (See *Provocative Recruitment Strategies from Industry*, for some interesting examples). Regardless of the techniques used, though, it is essential that the recruiting effort be specific and directed by the concern's strategic vision and culture. In this fashion, an organization can attract staff members who not only meet the enterprise's future needs but will harmonize well within the enterprise's evolving management structure.

See It in Action

Provocative Recruitment Strategies from Industry

Sure, any organization can use conventional means like home page postings, job fairs, employee referrals, and college relations to recruit talent, but in a tight job market these approaches generally yield huge pools of the wrong type of applicant. Yes, there will be "gold nuggets" in the bunch; however, it will take a lot of sifting to find them.

Indeed, it takes a different approach, and some creativity, to reach the right kind of staffing candidate. Here is a sampling of some of the more innovative ways in which firms are recruiting talent these days:

✓ Restaurant chain **T.G.I. Fridays** captured the essence of their brand—pride, passion, personality—through an online community network called Fridoids used to recruit new employees. The goal of the community was to engage and project the culture of T.G.I. Fridays. The community has created an honest representation of the staff and a positive and genuine illustration of the brand, which helps candidates self-select and opt out if they don't feel a fit.[6]

✓ Video game company **Red 5 Studios** handpicked 100 ideal candidates and got to "know" them by researching their social media profiles and past work. The start-up then sent each one a personalized iPod equipped with a welcome from the CEO. More than 90 recipients responded to the pitch. Three left their jobs to come on board.[7]

✓ **Quicken Loans** conducted a "blitz" of local retail stores and restaurants, sending employees out to interact with workers and offer interviews to those who really stood out.[8]

✓ When opening its new Australian Mega Store, **IKEA** placed "Career Instructions" inside each of the company's signature flat-pack product boxes. When customers opened their newly purchased IKEA products, they had instructions on how to "assemble a future" with this highly successful Swedish company. The technique resulted in 280 new hires.[9]

✓ **MasterCard's** "Cashless Society" campaign yielded over 350 qualified applicants, compared to the 20–30 applications the company has traditionally received upon advertising a job. Applicants were asked to use a third-party social media site to explain what a "cashless society" meant to them, and were given four weeks to complete this challenge.[10]

✓ Professional service firm **PwC** is now building competitive games into the recruiting process in order to assess applicants in critical thinking, teamwork, and communication.[11]

Notice that, apart from the technique used, all of these more novel recruitment approaches included elements that emphasized "fit" with mission and culture. We can hedge the bet as it relates to hiring the best candidates, too, by using our enterprise's long-term vision as our guide.

ITEM 6: ATTRACT AND INCENTIVIZE WITH TRAINING

Undoubtedly, training is a critical aspect of organizational development. As discussed in Chapter 8, we must invest in continually improving our personnel's skills and competencies in order to ensure that our enterprises possess the human assets required to surpass customer expectations and meet the changing demands of the marketplace. But the provision of training can become increasingly more perplexing as we reimagine the organization.

The challenge comes with the realization that the workforce is becoming increasingly transient and that free agent workers are filling more critical roles than ever before. At first blush, these realities make it progressively more difficult to rationalize a large investment in training because the return on that investment can be so unclear when viewed through the myopic lens of direct cost versus payback.

However, when we apply a broader perspective on training's potential benefits to an organization by recognizing that it could be used to both attract and incentivize talent (internal staff and free agent, alike), then the investment looks especially solid. It enables the development of skills required now and those that will be essential to the enterprise in the future. Still not convinced? Consider these reasons to invest as well:

✓ Available talent may not be fully prepared to deliver what is needed. Therefore, training will be necessary to develop the skills required for immediate success (see *Staffing Challenge Lies Ahead*, for some interesting statistics that support this idea).

✓ The competition for qualified talent to fill essential roles will be increasingly stiff as highly competent people become less available, so a well-structured training program can be used to attract high-end talent to the organization.

✓ Training, especially that which is self-selected, can be used as a fine nonmonetary reward for staff who have gone above and beyond the call of duty (see Chapter 8, for more on this).

✓ Similarly, training rewards can be developed as an incentive for good performance. High-quality talent are always motivated by having the opportunities to learn and develop new skills and competencies.

✓ Many Generation Y workers will choose to be employed by more than one business at a time. Thus, provisions must be made to ensure that these free agents are trained in the organization's operating policies, procedures, and quality standards, so that they can assimilate quickly and deliver desired results. Providing them with additional skills-specific training will only serve to make them that much more productive.

Yes, there will be dollars allocated to develop skills among some personnel who may not provide payback over the long run, if they move on to other employers. However, as long as there is enough return to justify the investment in the short-run, then training both internal and free agent staff is still a good business decision. After all, the organization gains in goodwill and reputation, which will, in turn, attract better permanent employees and more highly qualified freelancers to the enterprise in the future.

See It in Action

Staffing Challenge Lies Ahead

In the not-too-distant future, there will, indeed, be a staffing problem in the United States. The Broad Foundation backs this assertion. The foundation's mission is to dramatically transform urban K-12 public education through better governance, management, labor relations, and competition. Here are some interesting statistics from one of their recent reports:[12]

✓ The United States spends over $885 billion annually on public education. But despite this investment, almost 30 percent of American students do not finish high school.
✓ The U.S. ranks twenty-first worldwide in mathematical literacy.
✓ The country ranks seventeenth worldwide in scientific literacy.
✓ It is fourteenth worldwide in reading literacy.
✓ Based on these rankings, it is no wonder that the United States also ranks second worldwide—behind Ireland—in terms of highest percentage of students who find school to be boring (at 61%).
✓ Meanwhile, by 2018, almost two-thirds of all US jobs will require some sort of postsecondary education.
✓ This translates into a need of some 22 million new workers with postsecondary degrees to fill those jobs.
✓ The US education system will produce just over 18 million postsecondary graduates in that time frame, resulting in a shortfall of over three million graduates.
✓ Sixty-three percent of life science and aerospace firms already report shortages of qualified workers.
✓ In the coming decade, 60 percent of the existing aerospace and defense workforce will reach retirement age.

Based on these findings, the US education system appears broken, and it doesn't look like it will fix itself. In fact, if fundamental reform isn't undertaken soon, it is very likely that US businesses will find themselves extremely short-handed in the coming years. Therefore, training of the American workforce should be a top priority for most executives in the United States.

CHECKLIST ITEM 7: RETAIN THROUGH INNO-
VATIVE WORK SETTING CHANGES

As previously mentioned, the next generation of worker has a strong desire for independence and lifestyle freedom, so they are likely to continue to seek out free agency as a means to gain more control over the ways in which they work. While operating models can be adjusted to better accommodate the influx and outflow of talent to the organization as needed, retaining personnel should still be managed as a priority because:

✓ key knowledge losses are amplified with high employee turnover
  rates;
✓ training investments can be squandered when staff leave for better
  opportunities;
✓ work disruptions, brought on by turnover, can diminish quality;
✓ the customer experience can be distressed when key workers
  move on;
✓ business retention can be negatively impaired if customers move their
  business to follow key workers;
✓ employee morale can be upset, if turnover is rampant.

Indeed, if we're not careful, regular turnover can wreak havoc on an organization, unless we begin to forge innovative work settings that satisfy Gen Y's personal needs.

Here are some ideas that may resonate with the Millennial workforce:

✓ concierge services (e.g., car   ✓ ability to work remotely
  maintenance, dry cleaning, etc.)   ✓ flex-time
✓ on-premises child day care   ✓ casual dress code
✓ on-premises pet care   ✓ job rotation programs
✓ ownership opportunities   ✓ periodic paid sabbaticals

These approaches are worth considering because they will persuade some of the next generation workforce to commit to the organization— one that demonstrates a willingness to create a comfortable and rewarding work setting for its staff members.

CHECKLIST ITEM 8: REEXAMINE THE VENDOR CONNECTION

The redefining of the way in which vendors "fit" into the enterprise is the last piece of reimagining the organization. Vendors can play an important role in enabling organizations of the future to be more *"mutable"*—that is, able to scale to size and capacity as needed. We have already seen countless examples of how outsourcing repetitive activities to best-of-breed vendors is a way for an organization to better manage business cycle fluctuations, while enhancing their capabilities to meet market demands for speed and flexibility.

The next iteration of reexamining the vendor connection may involve going back to the future—back to a time in which products and services were exchanged among providers and cooperative selling practices led to new strategic alliances that opened up fresh markets for member "partners." Reexamining vendor relationships in this way may not only lead to more organizational suppleness and enhanced capabilities but can also be central to extending market reach.

For example, a cash-strapped spare parts manufacturer to the aerospace industry used a job shop to provide anodized coatings on its finished product before delivery to its primary customers. But after entering into a reciprocal agreement with the coating company, the manufacturer now gets its coatings at no charge in exchange for producing a part that the coating company can coat and resell to a medical device manufacturer. The spare parts company solves a cash flow problem and the coatings company grows its market reach—everyone wins!

These kinds of exchanges will likely evolve as firms become flatter and leaner. Accordingly, we will have to think differently about our operations and the vendor connection in order to identify the potential for shifting the organization's business relationships. However, by doing so, we are likely to create new opportunities to leverage future vendor / strategic partner dynamics to better shape and grow our enterprises.

TO CLOSE

Organizations can no longer afford to be top-heavy. Management bureaucracies destroy productivity and milk the creative juices out of even the most ambitious staff member, which allows lethargy and sluggishness to seep into the culture and kill the enterprise. A flatter organizational design coupled with a team-based operating model is needed to empower and motivate staff to do their best.

Personnel at all levels of the concern must be trained in the fundamentals of team-based management. Related human resource management procedures aimed at attracting, recruiting, training, and retaining staff must be adjusted to accommodate this new way of being organized, while the executive team reexamines free-agent and vendor relationships and seeks out more imaginative ways to grow and evolve the enterprise.

The marketplace rewards speed and agility. Therefore, nothing is more important than ensuring that the reimagined organization is remodeled to be a solid expressway to the future.

A BOLD VISION FOR TOMORROW'S ORGANIZATIONS

Thoughts are but dreams till their effects be tried.

—William Shakespeare

Before we part, let me leave you with one last *thought piece* to consider as you begin to use the ***The Executive Checklist*** to lead your organization into the future. It is intended to provide a universal vision of what can be achieved by adopting the ideas offered in the book:

Leadership is the foundation for change. It has been
established in tomorrow's organization.

Outstanding leadership has been established. It conveys a very strong sense of being "in it together" among the people who work within tomorrow's organization. The executive team collaborates with, and includes, staff in problem-solving and issues resolution. The best of the bunch don't pretend to have all of the answers. Rather, they prefer to solicit input and perspectives from the front-line personnel who do the work every day.

Trust is a vital component of enduring achievement. Time has
been spent to build it within tomorrow's organization.

Providing strength against adversity within the enterprise, the high-trust work setting that has been established is efficient and resilient. All the focus is on results and not on each other. People just seem to pull together—to be willing to directly address problems as they arise. No excuses are made or expected in tomorrow's organization.

The vision for tomorrow's organization has been translated into action through the development of a strategic plan.

It is very easy for today's executive teams to get distracted by the speed of change and velocity at which information comes hurtling at them. However, a solid strategic plan and a set of sound processes required to support its evolution have been established. The tendency to blindly chase any new idea that holds promise has diminished because the strategic plan acts as an evaluation screen that helps the organization of tomorrow retain its focus and avoid squandering its resources on ideas that don't enable the achievement of the vision.

The staff of tomorrow's organization has been engaged. Their support has accelerated success.

By making a conscientious effort to engage staff in their transformation efforts, the leaders of tomorrow's organization enable hale and hearty work environments to take seed and propagate—indeed, establishing environments in which individual strengths are not only acknowledged but are capitalized upon, and in which every staff member has the opportunity to display his or her talents and contribute to the achievement of the strategic vision of the organization.

Work is managed through a portfolio of projects within tomorrow's organization. It is a means to strategic alignment.

A project portfolio provides a context for simplifying the complex. Therefore, it makes perfect sense for the executive team in tomorrow's organization to arrange all of the work necessary to realize its strategic vision into a project portfolio. By doing so, the enterprise has the capacity to break larger endeavors into smaller ones that are more easily managed. The portfolio provides a framework that enables executive engagement in project execution and delivers a platform for informed decision-making—ensuring proper resource allocation and improved management and monitoring of the internal investments needed to achieve long-term business success.

*The management team of tomorrow's organization renovated
its business as a way to become "of Choice."*

Whether stated deliberately, or otherwise, every executive wants his or her
organization to be "of Choice," which translates into becoming the Organization of Choice, Employer of Choice, and Investment of Choice within their
enterprise's niche, market, and industry. To be "Of Choice" underpins virtually every strategic initiative that the management team of tomorrow's
organization imagines, staffs, funds, and executes. It continually renovates its
business operations to ensure it.

*Tomorrow's organization has seamlessly integrated its
technology because it is at the core of all that it does.*

It is critical to note that the technology decisions made today are indispensably central to the long-term health of the enterprise. Accordingly, the executive team at tomorrow's organization has stopped conceding technology
decision-making responsibility to technologists and have begun to expand
their own awareness and understanding of the possibilities that today's technologies enable, so that they can devise strategies to better exploit these and
future technological capabilities required to fulfill their organization's strategic vision.

*The staff at tomorrow's organization has been transformed,
too. It is the "People Part" of enterprise-wide change.*

Staff transformation is about creating a management structure that trains,
measures, and rewards personnel for delivering desired outcomes. By enabling
employees to succeed and rewarding them when they do, the management
team at tomorrow's organization has continually expanded staff capabilities,
generating sought-after results and nurturing innovative ways of conducting
the business of the enterprise.

*Communications practices have been renewed at tomorrow's
organization because transparency improves performance.*

In the end, communication is a competence that every organization must
develop in order to stay sharp, remain focused, and be better positioned to
readily seize marketplace opportunities as they arise. A communications

renewal program that embraces new ideas and theories on how tomorrow's organization communicates not only improves the enterprise's communications competence but enables a more open work environment to emerge—one that values active participation of its employees and increases their sense of being in it together.

Tomorrow's organization has been reimagined, opening an expressway to the future.

Organizations can no longer afford to be top-heavy. Management bureaucracies destroy productivity and milk the creative juices out of even the most ambitious staff member, which allows lethargy and sluggishness to seep into the culture and kill the enterprise. A flatter organizational design coupled with a team-based operating model has been adopted in tomorrow's organization. It empowers and motivates staff to do their best.

AND, WITH THAT . . .

We have covered a lot of ground together between these pages. We've explored a great variety of thoughts and ideas about setting direction and managing change. We've learned how executives are already leveraging some of the concepts discussed to improve their enterprises. I hope that you choose to use these concepts to make a difference in your organization, as well.

Indeed, it is time to begin to do the work needed to realize a bold and exhilarating, new vision for our organizations. Let's be sure to use *The Executive Checklist* as our guide.

So long, for now!

A LAST WORD

If you like the book that you just read and are interested in instituting *The Executive Checklist* framework within your organization, I have developed a formal program that can help you to do that. The program will lead you and your organization through a process of evaluating where it is in terms of each of *The Executive Checklist's* ten main checkpoints and helping you develop an action plan tailored to your enterprise's specific needs. The program consists of three major elements:

1. **Pre-Workshop Baseline Survey** (1 Day)—which helps you gather and evaluate the right information about your organization's current state;
2. **Executive Checklist Workshop** (3 Days)—which helps you determine the actions needed to bridge the gap between your current state and where you want to bring the organization in the future, which in turn culminates in the creation of an *Executive Checklist Action Plan*; and
3. **Post-Workshop Recommendation Clinic** (1 Day)—which helps you fine-tune the projects and programs that were identified and developed for your organization's *Executive Checklist Action Plan*.

If this sounds like something that can help you drive needed change in your enterprise, then please visit *www.best-practices-group.com* for more information or send me a note at *jkerr@ best-practices-group.com* to schedule a time to talk.

ABOUT THE AUTHOR

James M. Kerr is a management consultant and organizational behaviorist. He specializes in strategic planning, corporate transformation, and project and program development. For over 20 years, Jim has forged a different type of consulting practice—one that does its engagements "with" its clients, instead of "to" them.

Whether helping larger organizations, like The Home Depot, reimagine its store operations, or advising smaller firms, like specialty insurer Jewelers Mutual, open up new markets, Jim has a reputation for making a difference.

A recognized thought leader, Jim continues to provide cutting-edge solutions to his clients through a strong dedication to research and study. *The Executive Checklist* is Jim's fourth business strategy book. It is a testament to his commitment to helping leaders improve the ways in which they guide and shape their organizations.

For more information about Jim or his management consulting practice, please visit **www.best-practices-group.com** or send a note directly to him at *jkerr@ best-practices-group.com.*

NOTES

CHAPTER 2

1. "Ten Hallmarks of High-trust Organizations" by Robert Whipple, *Leading Edge Online Journal*, www.roberts.edu, Roberts Wesleyan College, Volume 4, Number 1, April 2011.
2. Stephen M. R. Covey, *The Speed of Trust: The One Thing That Changes Everything* (New York: The Free Press, 2006), p. 139.
3. *"Firms resist New pay Equity Rules,"* by Leslie Kwoh, *Wall Street Journal*, http://online.wsj.com, June 26, 2012.
4. *"Whole Foods' Mackey Says Employees Should Come before Investors," by Brooke Sutherland, Bloomberg, January 18, 2013.*
5. "Causal Impact of Employee Work Perceptions on the Bottom Line of Organizations," by James K. Harter, Frank L. Schmidt, James W. Asplund, Emily A. Killham, and Sangeeta Agrawal, *Perspectives on Psychological Science, July 2010, vol. 5, pp. 378 – 389.*
6. http://www.dreamworksanimation.com/insidedwa/ourculture
7. http://www.plantemoran.com/about/media/2011/Pages/still-jerk-free-pm-named-to-fortune-magazines-list-of-100-best-companies-to-work-for-for-13th-consecutive-year.aspx

CHAPTER 4

1. Derived, in part, from *"Gen Y and the 2020 Organization,"* by James M. Kerr, Management Issues, www.management-issues.com, January 17, 2011.
2. *The Best Practices Enterprise*, by James M. Kerr, J. Ross Publishing, 2006, pp. 172–174.

CHAPTER 5

1. *"Marriott Gains New Edge in Project Transparency, Planning,"* by Hewlett-Packard Development Company, L.P., http://h20195.www2.hp.com/V2/GetDocument.aspx?docname=4AA3–8543ENW&cc=us&lc=en, July, 2012, p.2.
2. *American Heritage® Dictionary of the English Language*, Houghton Mifflin, as available online at http://education.yahoo.com/reference/dictionary/entry/artifact, March 7, 2013.
3. "The Ten Commandments of Project Management," by James M. Kerr, *Computerworld*, www.computerworld.com, October 2, 2006.

CHAPTER 6

1. *The Best Practices Enterprise*, by James M. Kerr, J. Ross Publishing, 2006, p. 17.

CHAPTER 7

1. *Gartner Says By 2015, More Than 50 Percent of Organizations That Manage Innovation Processes Will Gamify Those Processes,* Press Release, Gartner Inc., April 12, 2011.
2. "Success Story: Golden State Foods," Computer Sciences Corporation, February 17, 2012, p.2.
3. "*CASE STUDY: Infrastructure-as-a-Service Transforms Fujitsu's UK Operations,*" Fujitsu Limited, http://www.fujitsu.com/uk/Images/fujitsu-iaas.pdf, September 2010.
4. "*Vail Resorts Creates Epic Experiences with Customer Intelligence,*" SAS Institute, Inc., July 26, 2012, p.4

CHAPTER 8

1. "*A $1 Billion 'Model' Employee Education Program,*" by Steve Lohr, NY Times Bits Blog, January 31, 2012.
2. "Beam Inc. Reinvents Total Rewards to Support a New Global Culture," By Lucie P. Lawrence, Strategy at Work, towerswatson.com, November 2012.
3. "*Why 'Good Jobs' Are Good for Retailers,*" by Zeynep Ton, Harvard Business Review, January-February 2012.
4. "*Study Reveals Global Creativity Gap,*" Adobe Systems, Inc. Press Release, www.adobe.com, April 23, 2012.

CHAPTER 9

1. 2012 CEO.com Social CEO Report, published by CEO.com, p. 4, August 3, 2012.
2. EA Makes Worst Company in American History, Wins Title for Second Year in A Row!, by Chris Morran, www.consumerist.com, April 9, 2013.
3. "*INSIDE JCPENNEY: Widespread Fear, Anxiety, and Distrust Of Ron Johnson and His New Management Team,*" by *Kim Bhasin, Business Insider, February 22, 2013.*
4. Philips Advocates Board-Level Global Collaboration, by Cisco Systems, Inc., http://www.cisco.com/en/US/prod/collateral/ps7060/ps8329/ps9573/royal_philips_electronics.pdf, September 7, 2012, page 2.

CHAPTER 10

1. "*Who's the Boss? There Isn't One,*" by Rachel Emma Silverman, *The Wall Street Journal,* http://online.wsj.com/home-page, June 19, 2012.
2. http://www.gore.com/en_xx/aboutus/culture/
3. http://www.slideshare.net/thetalentproject/the-free-agent-workforce
4. http://www.valvesoftware.com/company/people.html
5. "*Valve Corp., The Boss-Less Company Where Employees Run The Ship,*" by Drew Guarini, The Huffington Post, June 20, 2012.
6. "*Recruitment lessons from AT&T & TGI Fridays,*" by Pierce Boylin, www.recruiterbox.com, August 2012.
7. "10 Creative Recruiting Strategies for Finding Great Hires," by Bianca Male, www.businessinsider.com, February 25, 2010.
8. Ibid.
9. "5 Reasons IKEA's Australian Recruitment Campaign is Brilliant," by Melany Gallant, www.halogensoftware.com, February 22, 2012.

10. "The Death of the Resume: Five Ways To Re-Imagine Recruiting," by Jeane Meister, www.forbes.com, July 23, 2012.
11. Ibid.
12. "*Statistics: Our Public Education Is in Deep Distress,*" by The Broad Foundation, as provided on www.broadeducation.org/about/crisis_stats.html on May 16, 2012.

INDEX

A

Aceto, Peter, 172
Adams, John Quincy, 5
Adobe Systems, Inc., 167–8
Akerson, Dan, 172
Alvarez & Marsal, 47
Amazon, 140
American Management Association
    (AMA), 154
AmSurg, 100–101
Apple, 80, 111, 140
artifacts, 98–101
Athletes' Performance, Inc., 122–4
automation, 122–4

B

Bacon, Francis, 109
bad leaders, 19–21
Barker, Sean, 143
baselines, 57–8, 133–6, 171, 213
Beam, Inc., 162–3
behaviors, new, 61–2
Belichick, Bill, 35–6
Blake, William, 67
blogging, 74, 171–3, 185–6
Brady, Tom, 36
Branson, Richard, 22–3
Bush, George W., 129
business blind spots, 62–4
business principles, 54–7
Business Process as a Service (BPaaS),
    137, 145
business renovation, 211
    and automation, 122–4
    Business Renovation Checklist, 110
    center of excellence (CoE), 125–6
    choosing an approach for, 115–17
    and differentiation, 110–12

and location dependencies, 120–22
and making it last, 124–8
and silo mentality, 118–20
and strategic planning, 112–15
and the whole process, 117–18

C

Challenger space shuttle, 25
checklists
    Business Renovation Checklist, 110
    Communications Renewal
        Checklist, 170
    Executive Checklist, 3
    introduction to, 1–4
    Leadership Establishment Checklist, 6
    Organization Reimagination
        Checklist, 189–90
    Project Portfolio Management
        Checklist, 88
    Staff Engagement Checklist, 68
    Staff Transformation Checklist, 150
    Strategy-setting Checklist, 45
    Technology Integration Checklist, 130
    Trust-building Checklist, 26
CIGNA HealthCare, 13–15
Cisco Telepresence, 179
Clarus Marketing Group, 80–1
Cleary, Rosemary, 119
cloud computing, 104, 131, 136–7,
    139–41, 148
collaboration, 15–17, 177–9
common artifacts, 98–101
common language, 95–8
communication, 211–12
    and collaboration, 177–9
    Communications Renewal
        Checklist, 170
    drive-by, 183–4

communication—*Continued*
  early and frequent, 10–12
  framework, 69–70
  and informal networks, 182–3
  and leadership, 184–7
  and middle layer of management,
    175–7
  open door, 183–4
  scope of, 170–3
  and simplification, 180–2
  and Thoreau, 180–2
  and transparency, 173–5
competitive advantage vs. table stakes,
  139–42
Computer Sciences Corporation
  (CSC), 141
Connecticut's Department of Revenue
  Services (DRS), 49–50, 106–7,
  119–20
Corning, 112
Costco, 163–5
Covey, Stephen, 30
creativity, 19, 40, 50–1, 165–8, 194, 201
Cummins, Inc., 126–8

D
Deming, W. Edwards, 116
differentiation, 110–12
direction, actively setting, 8–10
Disciple Model, 186
diversity, 17–19, 63, 74, 81–3
doing your best, 37
doing your job, 34–6
Domino's Pizza, 138
Donigan, Heyward, 14
dreaming the dream, 6–8, 23
DreamWorks Animation, 17, 40–1
DuPont, 112
dynamic involvement, 12–15

E
early adopters, 74–6
Edelman, 31–2
Edison, Thomas, 87
Einstein, Albert, 189
Electronic Arts (EA), 174–5
engage, deciding to, 68–72
  see also staff engagement
EpicMix, 145–7
excuse-making, 22–3, 26, 210
execution, *see* business renovation

executive blogs, 74, 171–3, 185–6
Executive Checklist, 3
  see also checklists

F
Federal Deposit Insurance Corporation
  (FDIC), 131–3
Forbes Insights, 17–19
Ford, 140
Fortune Brands, 112
freelancers, 194–7, 203
Fujitsu, 142–5

G
gamesmanship behavior, 32–4
gamification, 137–9, 145–8
General Electric (GE), 112, 116, 178,
  191–2
Generation Y, 46, 51, 68, 77–81, 155,
  195, 203
Glazer, Jeffrey, 61
Golden State Foods (GSF), 141–2
Goldstein, Adam, 172
Google, 73–4, 129
Gore, Bill, 193–4
Gore, Genevieve, 193–4

H
Half, Robert, 32–4
H&M, 121–2
Harry & David, 47–8
Hartford, The, 186–7
Home Depot, 2, 57, 140

I
IBM, 2, 112
ideology, new, 46–51
IKEA, 201
inclusiveness, 17–19, 63, 74, 81–3
independence, 19, 50–1, 136, 144, 155,
  195, 205
  see also location dependencies
Infrastructure as a Service (IaaS), 137,
  143–5
Insurity, 61
integrated administration, 94–5
Integrity Insurance, 55–7
Internet of Things, 136, 144
Ishikawa, Kaoru, 116
IT, *see* technology
IT baseline, 133–6

J
Jacoby, Darren, 146
JCPenney, 176–7
jerk-free policy, 42–3
Jobs, Steve, 16
Jongedijk, Jap, 178–9
JPMorgan Chase, 97–8
Juran, Joseph M., 116

K
keeping it light, 39–41
Kelly Services, Inc., 195–7
Krater, Gordon, 42

L
leadership
   and bad leaders, 19–21
   and blind spots, 62–3
   and collaboration, 17
   and communication, 10–12, 173–4,
      183–7, 193–4, 198
   and dynamic coaching, 12–15
   and excuses, 22–3
   as foundation for change, 5, 209
   and having a dream, 6–8
   and inclusiveness, 17–19
   and IT, 147–8
   and modeling behavior, 26–9, 32–4,
      173, 175, 184
   new paradigm of, 47
   product, 140, 142
   and setting direction, 8–10
   and sharing the wealth, 37–8
   and staff engagement, 67–70
   thought, 125
   and vision, 6–8, 22–3
Leadership Establishment Checklist, 6
Lean, 115–16, 126
LexisNexis, 6–7, 52–3
Lincoln, Abraham, 45
location dependencies, 79, 120–2

M
Mackenzie, Mindy, 162
Mackey, John, 38–9
management huddles, 9–10
Marriott, 82–3, 90–1, 172
Marriott, Bill, 172
MasterCard, 201
measurement and reward programs,
      83–6, 149, 157–63

Microsoft, 101, 138
Millennials, *see* Generation Y
Miller, Dana, 127–8
mobile computing, 129–31, 136,
      144, 146
modeling behavior, 26–9
Molex, 75–6
Monsanto, 112

N
National Collegiate Athletic Association
      (NCAA), 27–8
National Football League, 35–6
Netflix, 140
Nietzsche, Friedrich, 25
Nike, 139–40
No Spin Zones, 29–32
Nokia, 112

O
"of Choice," 109–10, 128
   see also business renovation
organization reimagination, 212
   and challenges of alternative designs,
      197–9
   and freelancer models, 194–7
   and incentives, 202–4
   and networked designs, 192–4
   Organization Reimagination
      Checklist, 189–90
   and the pyramid structure, 190–2
   and recruitment, 199–204
   and retention, 205
   and strategic vision, 199–202
   and team-based designs, 192–4
   and training, 202–4
   and vendors, 206
   and work-setting changes, 205
O'Reilly, Bill, 29–30
organizational memory, 59–60
outside-in perspective, 46, 48–50, 84

P
Parsons, Bob, 173
Philips, 178–9
Pixar, 16–17
plan administration, 9, 49, 57–9, 94
Plante & Moran, 42–3
Platform as a Service (PaaS), 137, 141,
      144, 145
Plato, 1

Playboy, 139
project portfolio management
    (PPM), 210
  and common artifacts, 98–101
  and common language, 95–8
  initiating, 91–3
  and integrated administration, 94–5
  integrating with strategic planning
      processes, 93–4
  and knowing your starting point,
      88–91
  PPM Checklist, 88
  product offerings, 102–5
  ten commandments for, 105–7
  tools for, 101–5
promoting a new culture, 72–4
PwC, 202
Pyramid for Success, 27–9
pyramid organizational structure,
    190–2

Q
Quicken Loans, 201

R
radio frequency (RF) technology, 146–7
recruitment, 199–204
Red 5 Studios, 201
reward programs, see measurement and
    rewards programs
Roberts, Kevin, 173
Rodriguez, Ana, 76
Royal Philips Electronics, 178–9

S
Scott, Leslie, 90
Seiko, 64
Shakespeare, William, 209
shared training, 155–7
sharing the wealth, 37–9
Shaw, George Bernard, 169
Sias, Rhonda, 142
silos mentality, 118–20
Six Sigma, 115–16, 126
Slark, Martin, 76
SnapComm, 181–2
social media, 30–1, 51, 74, 79, 137, 145,
    146, 171–3, 186, 200–201
soft skills, 152–5
Software-as-a-Service (SaaS), 104, 131,
    136–7, 141, 144

Specific, Measureable, Achievable,
    Relevant, and Time-related
    (SMART) approach, 160–1
staff engagement, 210
  and deciding to engage, 68–72
  and early adopters, 74–6
  and Generation Y, 77–81
  and inclusion, 81–3
  and measurement and reward
      programs, 83–6
  and promoting a new culture, 72–4
  Staff Engagement Checklist, 68
staff transformation, 211
  and the big picture, 152–5
  and continuous execution, 150–2
  and creative teams, 165–8
  and incentives, 163–5
  and measurement, 149, 157–61, 165
  and outcomes, 158–61
  pillars of, 149–51, 165
  and program briefs, 151–2
  and rewards, 149, 161–3, 165
  and shared training, 155–7
  and soft skills, 152–5
  Staff Transformation Checklist, 150
  and training, 149–57
strategy planning, 45–6, 210
  and business blind spots, 62–4
  and business principles, 54–7
  and new behaviors, 61–2
  and new ideology, 46–51
  program for, 57–62
  and project portfolio management,
      93–4
  and technology, 130–3, 145–7
  and vision story, 51–4
Stress in Americasurvey, 77–8
subject matter experts (SMEs), 96
Sullivan, Kevin, 49
Swiss watchmaking industry, 64

T
table stakes vs. competitive advantage,
    139–42
technology, 211
  available, 136–9
  and competitive advantage, 139–42
  evolution of, 147–8
  and innovation, 142–5, 147–8
  and IT baseline, 133–6
  and strategic planning, 130–3, 145–7

Technology Integration Checklist, 130
  see also social media
Temkin Ratings, 15
T.G.I. Fridays, 201
Thoreau, Henry David, 149, 180–2
3M, 111
Ton, Zeynep, 165
Total Quality Management (TQM),
    115–16, 126
Toyota, 116
Trader Joe's, 165
training programs, 57, 149–57, 164–5,
    202–4
transparency, 2, 29–30, 169–70, 173–5,
    184–5, 187, 211–12
trust, 209–10
  and behavior modeling, 26–9
  and doing your best, 37
  and doing your job, 34–6
  and focusing on the outside, 29
  and gamesmanship behavior, 32–4
  and keeping it light, 39–41
  and No Spin Zones, 29–32
  and sharing the wealth, 37–9
  Trust-building Checklist, 26

U
Ullman, III, Myron E. (Mike), 177
United Technologies Corporation
    (UTC), 156–7

UPS, 140
US Army, 139

V
Vail Resorts, 145–7
Valve Corporation, 198–9
Virgin, 22–3
Vision Magazine, 7, 53
vision story, 45, 51–4
  see also dreaming the dream
Vision Trade Show, 6–7

W
Walker, Julie, 55
Walmart, 140, 163–5
Welch, Patrick, 13–14
Whirlpool Corporation, 153–5
Whole Foods Market, Inc., 38–9
Wipro Ltd., 181–2
W. L. Gore & Associates, Inc.,
    193–4
Wooden, John, 27–9
World at Work engagement study,
    85–6

X
Xerox, 112

Z
Zappos, 71–2